The Footprints of Colonialism: Tracing the Impact of Imperial Rule

Shah Rukh

Published by Shah Rukh, 2024.

While every precaution has been taken in the preparation of this book, the publisher assumes no responsibility for errors or omissions, or for damages resulting from the use of the information contained herein.

THE FOOTPRINTS OF COLONIALISM: TRACING THE IMPACT OF IMPERIAL RULE

First edition. August 8, 2024.

Copyright © 2024 Shah Rukh.

Written by Shah Rukh.

Table of Contents

Prologue..1

Chapter 1: The Scramble for Africa...3

Chapter 2: British Rule in India...6

Chapter 3: The Spanish Conquest of the Americas......................10

Chapter 4: French Colonization of Algeria..............................14

Chapter 5: Dutch East Indies Control.....................................19

Chapter 6: Portuguese Empire in Brazil..................................25

Chapter 7: Belgian Exploitation of the Congo........................30

Chapter 8: Italian Colonialism in Libya.................................35

Chapter 9: German Empire in Namibia...................................40

Chapter 10: British Rule in America..45

Chapter 11: Japanese Occupation of Korea.............................50

Chapter 12: British Colonialism in Australia..........................55

Chapter 13: French Influence in Vietnam................................60

Chapter 14: Russian Expansion into Siberia............................65

Chapter 15: Ottoman Control of the Balkans..........................70

Chapter 16: British Domination of Egypt................................74

Chapter 17: Spanish Rule in the Philippines............................79

Chapter 18: Dutch Colonization of South Africa.....................83

Chapter 19: French Presence in Morocco.................................87

Chapter 20: British Control of Kenya......................................92

Chapter 21: Portuguese Colonization of Angola.....................98

Chapter 22: Danish West Indies Governance..........................104

Chapter 23: British Influence in the Caribbean.....................110

Chapter 24: French Rule in Madagascar.................................116

Chapter 25: Italian Occupation of Eritrea..............................121

Chapter 26: German Colonization of Tanzania.......................125

Chapter 27: Belgian Rule in Rwanda......................................131

Chapter 28: Japanese Expansion into Manchuria....................136

Chapter 29: Spanish Colonization of Florida..........................141

Chapter 30: British Settlements in Canada..............................146

Chapter 31: French Colonization of Louisiana 152

Chapter 32: Dutch Rule in Suriname 157

Chapter 33: Portuguese Control of Macau.................................. 162

Chapter 34: British Influence in Hong Kong.............................. 168

Chapter 35: French Colonization of Quebec.............................. 174

Chapter 36: Swedish Colonization of Delaware 178

Chapter 37: Russian Colonization of Alaska 183

Chapter 38: Spanish Missions in California................................ 188

Chapter 39: British Rule in Cyprus 193

Chapter 40: French Colonial Rule in Syria................................ 199

Chapter 41: Dutch Colonization of New York 203

Chapter 42: Portuguese Presence in Mozambique...................... 207

Chapter 43: German Rule in Cameroon.................................... 212

Chapter 44: British Control of Malaya...................................... 216

Chapter 45: French Influence in Tunisia................................... 222

Chapter 46: Spanish Rule in Guatemala 228

Chapter 47: British Colonization of New Zealand 234

Chapter 48: Dutch Colonization of Taiwan 240

Chapter 49: Italian Colonization of Somalia 245

Chapter 50: British Influence in Fiji... 250

Epilogue.. 255

Prologue

Colonialism, with its long and complex history, has left an indelible mark on the world. From the bustling markets of Mumbai to the serene landscapes of Namibia, the echoes of imperial rule resonate across continents. This book, "The Footprints of Colonialism: Tracing the Impact of Imperial Rule," embarks on a journey to explore these echoes, examining how the forces of colonialism shaped nations, cultures, and lives.

Colonialism is often depicted in stark terms, as a force of exploitation and oppression, but its impact is multifaceted. It brought about significant changes in governance, economy, and society, often leaving a mixed legacy of progress and pain. The chapters ahead delve into unique cases, each illustrating a distinct facet of colonial rule. From the British Raj in India to the Spanish conquest of the Americas, from the Dutch control of the East Indies to the Portuguese influence in Brazil, these stories weave a rich tapestry of historical experiences.

The narrative of colonialism is not a simple one of conquerors and the conquered. It involves a complex interplay of power, resistance, adaptation, and change. Indigenous cultures and traditions often clashed with, but also adapted to, the ways of the colonizers. Economic systems were transformed, sometimes bringing prosperity, but more often, exploitation and inequality. The imposition of foreign rule sparked both collaboration and resistance, leading to a myriad of outcomes that continue to shape the modern world.

This prologue sets the stage for a deeper exploration of these themes. It invites readers to reflect on the lasting impact of colonialism, not just as a historical phenomenon but as a living legacy that continues to influence global politics, economics, and cultural identities. As we trace the footprints of colonialism, we uncover stories of resilience and adaptation, as well as tales of suffering and resistance. Each chapter offers a glimpse into the complexities of imperial rule and its enduring consequences.

As we embark on this journey, we acknowledge that the history of colonialism is a shared one. It is a history that belongs not only to the colonizers and the colonized but to all of humanity. Understanding this history is crucial for building a more just and equitable future. By examining the past, we can better appreciate the challenges and opportunities of the present, and work towards a world where the lessons of history guide us towards greater empathy, justice, and understanding.

Welcome to "The Footprints of Colonialism: Tracing the Impact of Imperial Rule." Let us begin this journey together, tracing the paths of history, and uncovering the stories that have shaped our world.

Chapter 1: The Scramble for Africa

The Scramble for Africa was a period of rapid colonization of the African continent by European powers during the late 19th century and early 20th century, fundamentally transforming the continent's political, social, and economic landscape. This era, often dated from the Berlin Conference of 1884-1885 to the outbreak of World War I in 1914, saw European countries carve up Africa with little regard for existing ethnic, cultural, and linguistic boundaries. The motivations behind this scramble were varied, driven by economic interests, geopolitical strategy, national prestige, and a sense of racial superiority and mission to "civilize" African peoples.

Economically, the Industrial Revolution had created a voracious appetite for raw materials, new markets, and investment opportunities. Africa, rich in resources such as rubber, gold, diamonds, and other minerals, presented an attractive target for European nations seeking to fuel their burgeoning industries. Additionally, Africa's vast lands were seen as potential agricultural zones to supply European markets with products like coffee, tea, and cotton. The economic dimension of the Scramble for Africa was thus driven by a desire to exploit these resources and integrate the African economy into the global capitalist system dominated by Europe.

Geopolitically, the colonization of Africa was a game of strategy and competition among European powers. Nations like Britain, France, Germany, Belgium, Italy, Portugal, and Spain were keen to expand their empires and assert their dominance on the global stage. The Berlin Conference of 1884-1885, convened by German Chancellor Otto von Bismarck, aimed to regulate the competition and prevent conflict among European powers by establishing rules for the partition of Africa. This conference, which notably excluded any African representatives, formalized the "rules of the game" and led to a race among European powers to claim African territories, often through treaties with African leaders who may not have fully understood the implications or were coerced into agreements.

The Scramble for Africa was also driven by a sense of national prestige and the desire to assert global power. Empire-building was seen as a measure of national greatness, and possessing vast overseas territories was a source of pride and a symbol of a nation's strength. This nationalist fervor was often accompanied by a belief in the racial superiority of Europeans and a paternalistic duty to "civilize" African societies, which were deemed backward and in need of Western intervention. This ideological justification for colonization was rooted in social Darwinism and the belief that European civilization was the pinnacle of human progress, which needed to be spread to "lesser" peoples.

The consequences of the Scramble for Africa were profound and far-reaching. The arbitrary borders drawn by European powers during this period laid the groundwork for future conflicts and political instability, as they often split ethnic groups or forced rival groups into the same political entities. These borders, with little regard for the complex tapestry of African ethnicities and cultures, have had lasting impacts on the continent's post-independence political landscape, contributing to numerous civil wars and regional conflicts.

Socially, colonial rule disrupted traditional societies and ways of life. European powers imposed new systems of governance, education, and religion, often undermining or destroying indigenous institutions and practices. The introduction of Western education and Christianity, while leading to some positive changes such as literacy and modern medical practices, also eroded African cultural identities and heritage. Colonial authorities often used divide-and-rule tactics, favoring certain ethnic groups over others, which sowed seeds of division and mistrust that have persisted long after the end of colonial rule.

Economically, the exploitation of Africa's resources primarily benefited European colonizers. Colonial economies were structured to serve the interests of the metropole, with infrastructure such as railways and ports developed mainly to extract and export raw materials rather than to promote internal economic development. African labor was often exploited through systems of forced labor, taxation, and cash crop production, leading to widespread impoverishment and underdevelopment. The introduction of cash crops also altered traditional agricultural practices, sometimes leading to food insecurity as subsistence farming was replaced by the cultivation of export-oriented crops.

Resistance to colonial rule was widespread, with numerous uprisings and revolts occurring across the continent. African leaders and communities employed various strategies to resist European domination, ranging from armed conflict to diplomatic negotiations. Notable resistance movements included the Zulu resistance against the British in South Africa, led by King Cetshwayo, and the resistance of the Herero and Nama peoples against German colonization in present-day Namibia. These movements, although ultimately suppressed, demonstrated the resilience and determination of African societies to defend their autonomy and way of life.

The legacy of the Scramble for Africa continues to shape the continent's present and future. The colonial period left a mixed legacy of modernity and trauma, progress and exploitation. While colonial infrastructure and institutions laid some foundations for modern states, the exploitative nature of colonialism also left deep scars, including economic dependency, political instability, and social divisions. The struggle for independence, which gained momentum after World War II, was a testament to the enduring spirit of African resilience and the desire for self-determination.

Chapter 2: British Rule in India

British rule in India, which lasted from 1858 to 1947, was a period marked by significant changes in the political, social, economic, and cultural landscape of the subcontinent. This era began with the fall of the Mughal Empire and the establishment of the British East India Company as a dominant force, eventually leading to direct control by the British Crown after the Revolt of 1857. The impact of British imperialism on India was profound and multifaceted, influencing the country's development in both positive and negative ways.

The British East India Company initially came to India in the early 17th century as a trading entity seeking to capitalize on the lucrative spice trade. Over time, the company expanded its influence, leveraging military strength and strategic alliances to establish control over vast territories. By the mid-18th century, following key victories such as the Battle of Plassey in 1757 and the Battle of Buxar in 1764, the company had effectively become the de facto ruler of significant parts of India. The company exercised its power through a complex system of governance, employing a combination of direct administration and alliances with local rulers who became subsidiary allies.

The Revolt of 1857, also known as the Indian Rebellion or the Sepoy Mutiny, was a major turning point in British rule in India. Sparked by widespread discontent among Indian soldiers in the British army, the rebellion spread rapidly, drawing in diverse segments of Indian society dissatisfied with British policies and practices. Although the revolt was ultimately suppressed, it led to significant changes in British administration. The British Crown took direct control of India, marking the beginning of the British Raj. Queen Victoria was proclaimed Empress of India in 1876, symbolizing the formal incorporation of India into the British Empire.

Under the British Raj, the administration was centralized and bureaucratized. A new system of governance was established, with the

Viceroy serving as the representative of the British Crown and the head of the colonial administration. The Indian Civil Service (ICS) became the backbone of this administration, staffed predominantly by British officials, although a small number of Indians were later admitted. The British introduced legal reforms, codifying laws and establishing a judiciary that sought to impose uniform legal standards across the diverse and complex Indian society. However, these reforms often clashed with traditional Indian customs and practices, leading to social tensions.

Economically, British rule had a profound impact on India. The colonial economy was restructured to serve the interests of Britain, leading to significant changes in agricultural and industrial practices. The British promoted the cultivation of cash crops such as indigo, tea, cotton, and opium, which were exported to British markets. This shift disrupted traditional agricultural practices and often led to food shortages and famines, as farmers were compelled to grow cash crops instead of food staples. The most devastating famine during British rule was the Bengal Famine of 1943, which resulted in the deaths of an estimated three million people.

The British also invested in infrastructure development, constructing extensive networks of railways, roads, and telegraphs. These developments facilitated the extraction and transportation of raw materials, but they also had the unintended consequence of fostering economic integration and political unity among disparate regions of India. The introduction of modern industries, such as textiles and mining, led to the growth of urban centers and the rise of a new middle class. However, Indian industries faced stiff competition from British goods, leading to the decline of traditional crafts and industries.

Socially and culturally, British rule brought significant changes to Indian society. The British introduced Western education, which created a new class of educated Indians familiar with European ideas of democracy, liberty, and nationalism. Prominent figures such as Raja

Ram Mohan Roy and Ishwar Chandra Vidyasagar emerged as social reformers, advocating for changes in practices like sati, child marriage, and caste discrimination. The spread of English as a medium of instruction and administration also facilitated the emergence of a pan-Indian identity and the growth of nationalist sentiments.

Religiously, British rule had a complex impact on India. While the British generally pursued a policy of religious neutrality, their actions sometimes inadvertently fueled religious tensions. For instance, the introduction of new laws and practices often clashed with Hindu and Muslim religious traditions, leading to resistance and unrest. Missionary activities, although limited, also contributed to religious tensions as they sought to convert Indians to Christianity. The British often exploited religious and caste divisions to maintain control, a tactic known as "divide and rule," which sowed seeds of communal discord that would later culminate in the partition of India.

The rise of Indian nationalism was a direct response to British rule. The Indian National Congress, founded in 1885, became the primary platform for political expression and agitation against British policies. Initially, the Congress sought to achieve greater representation for Indians within the colonial administration and more autonomy for Indian provinces. However, the movement gradually radicalized, especially under the leadership of figures like Bal Gangadhar Tilak, who advocated for self-rule (Swaraj) and mobilized mass protests against British authority.

The early 20th century saw the emergence of Mohandas Karamchand Gandhi as the leader of the Indian independence movement. Gandhi's philosophy of nonviolent resistance (Satyagraha) and civil disobedience galvanized millions of Indians to participate in nationwide campaigns against British rule. Key events such as the Non-Cooperation Movement (1920-1922), the Salt March (1930), and the Quit India Movement (1942) mobilized vast sections of Indian society and drew international attention to India's struggle for independence. Gandhi's emphasis on nonviolence and his ability to unite people across religious, regional, and social divides made him a central figure in the nationalist movement.

The period leading up to independence was marked by intense political negotiations and communal tensions. The demand for a separate Muslim state led by the All India Muslim League and its leader, Muhammad Ali Jinnah, resulted in the eventual partition of India. The partition of 1947 created the separate nations of India and Pakistan, leading to one of the largest and most tragic migrations in human history. Millions of people were displaced, and widespread communal violence resulted in the deaths of hundreds of thousands.

The legacy of British rule in India is complex and multifaceted. On one hand, British colonialism brought about significant infrastructural development, modernization, and the introduction of democratic ideals. On the other hand, it also led to economic exploitation, social disruption, and deep-seated communal divisions. The struggle for independence and the eventual achievement of sovereignty in 1947 were testaments to the resilience and determination of the Indian people to reclaim their nation and shape their own destiny.

Post-independence, India faced the enormous challenge of nation-building, dealing with the legacy of colonial rule while striving to create a democratic, secular, and inclusive society. The institutions and infrastructure inherited from the British provided a foundation, but the country had to address the deep-rooted issues of poverty, illiteracy, and social inequality. The leaders of independent India, guided by the vision of figures like Jawaharlal Nehru, worked towards establishing a modern state while preserving the rich cultural and historical heritage of the subcontinent.

Chapter 3: The Spanish Conquest of the Americas

The Spanish Conquest of the Americas, initiated in the late 15th and early 16th centuries, stands as one of the most transformative and tumultuous periods in world history. This era saw the collision of vastly different civilizations, leading to profound changes in the social, political, and economic landscapes of both the Americas and Europe. The conquest began with Christopher Columbus's voyages and continued with the campaigns of conquistadors such as Hernán Cortés and Francisco Pizarro, ultimately leading to the establishment of Spanish colonial rule over large portions of the Americas.

The conquest was driven by a combination of factors, including the quest for wealth, the desire for national prestige, and religious zeal. The late 15th century was a period of burgeoning exploration as European powers sought new trade routes and territories. Spain, newly unified under Ferdinand II of Aragon and Isabella I of Castile, was eager to compete with Portugal, which had already made significant inroads into Africa and Asia. Columbus's first voyage in 1492, sponsored by the Spanish monarchs, marked the beginning of Spain's ventures into the New World. Although Columbus believed he had found a new route to Asia, his voyages opened up the Americas to European exploration and conquest.

One of the most significant early conquests was that of the Aztec Empire in present-day Mexico. Hernán Cortés arrived in 1519 with a small force of Spanish soldiers and a contingent of indigenous allies who were discontent with Aztec rule. The Aztec Empire, ruled by Moctezuma II, was a highly sophisticated and powerful civilization, with its capital, Tenochtitlan, situated on the site of modern-day Mexico City. Cortés and his men were initially welcomed by Moctezuma, but tensions soon escalated. Utilizing superior military technology, strategic alliances with local tribes, and exploiting internal dissensions, Cortés captured Tenochtitlan in 1521 after a brutal siege, effectively toppling the Aztec Empire.

The conquest of the Inca Empire in South America followed a similar pattern. Francisco Pizarro, inspired by the tales of wealth in the Andes, embarked on an expedition in 1532. The Inca Empire, under the rule of Atahualpa, was already weakened by a recent civil war and the spread of European diseases like smallpox, which had devastated the population even before Pizarro's arrival. Pizarro captured Atahualpa during a surprise attack in the city of Cajamarca and subsequently executed him after extracting a vast ransom of gold and silver. By 1533, Pizarro had taken the Inca capital, Cuzco, and established Spanish control over the region.

The Spanish conquests were characterized by their brutality and the devastating impact on indigenous populations. The introduction of European diseases, such as smallpox, measles, and influenza, to which the native populations had no immunity, led to catastrophic mortality rates. It is estimated that millions of indigenous people died as a result of these diseases, significantly reducing the population and weakening social structures. The encomienda system, established by the Spanish to organize labor, further exploited the surviving indigenous people, forcing them into labor on plantations and in mines under often inhumane conditions. This system effectively institutionalized the economic exploitation and social hierarchy that would define much of Spanish colonial rule.

Economically, the conquest had significant implications for both the Americas and Europe. The vast wealth extracted from the New World, particularly in the form of precious metals like gold and silver, had a transformative effect on the European economy. The influx of silver from the mines of Potosí in present-day Bolivia, for example, played a crucial role in fueling the economic expansion of Spain and other European powers, contributing to the broader process of global economic integration often referred to as the "Columbian Exchange." This period saw the exchange of goods, crops, animals, and technologies between the Old and New Worlds, profoundly altering diets, economies, and cultures on both sides of the Atlantic.

Socially and culturally, the Spanish conquest led to the creation of a new, hybrid society in the Americas. Spanish settlers, missionaries, and soldiers intermarried with indigenous populations, leading to the emergence of a mestizo (mixed) culture that blended European and native elements. The Spanish introduced their language, religion, and customs, while also adopting some aspects of indigenous cultures. The Catholic Church played a central role in this cultural transformation, establishing missions and converting large numbers of indigenous people to Christianity. This religious conversion was often enforced and accompanied by the suppression of native religions and practices, yet it also led to the syncretic blending of Christian and indigenous beliefs and rituals.

The legal and administrative structures of Spanish colonial rule were formalized through institutions like the viceroyalties, which were large administrative divisions governed by viceroys appointed by the Spanish Crown. The Viceroyalty of New Spain, established in 1535, covered much of North America, while the Viceroyalty of Peru, established in 1542, governed Spanish South America. These viceroyalties were further divided into audiencias (judicial districts) and corregimientos (administrative districts), creating a complex bureaucracy designed to maintain control over vast territories and diverse populations. The Spanish Crown also implemented the Laws of the Indies, a set of regulations intended to govern the behavior of colonists and protect the rights of indigenous people, though these laws were often poorly enforced and ignored by colonial authorities.

The Spanish conquest also had significant environmental impacts. The introduction of European agricultural practices, livestock, and crops transformed the landscape of the Americas. Spanish colonists established large haciendas (estates) and plantations, cultivating crops such as sugarcane, wheat, and coffee for export. The introduction of livestock such as cattle, horses, and sheep had far-reaching effects on the environment and indigenous ways of life, as these animals often disrupted local ecosystems and competed with native species. The exploitation of natural resources, particularly through mining, led to significant environmental degradation, including deforestation, soil erosion, and water pollution.

Resistance to Spanish rule was widespread and took various forms, ranging from armed rebellions to subtle forms of cultural resistance. Indigenous leaders such as Tupac Amaru II in Peru and Po'pay in New Mexico led significant uprisings against Spanish authorities, although these were ultimately suppressed. Many indigenous communities also engaged in everyday forms of resistance, preserving their languages, traditions, and cultural practices despite efforts to assimilate them into Spanish colonial society. Over time, these acts of resistance contributed to the development of distinct regional identities and the eventual movements for independence that would emerge in the 19th century.

The legacy of the Spanish conquest of the Americas is complex and enduring. On one hand, it led to the creation of new societies and cultures that continue to shape the Americas today. The Spanish language, Catholic religion, and numerous cultural practices introduced during the colonial period remain integral to the identity of many Latin American countries. On the other hand, the conquest also left a legacy of exploitation, inequality, and cultural disruption that continues to impact indigenous communities and broader societal structures. The history of the Spanish conquest is thus a story of both creation and destruction, of profound change and enduring continuity.

Chapter 4: French Colonization of Algeria

The French colonization of Algeria, which began in 1830 and lasted until Algeria's independence in 1962, represents one of the most significant and contentious episodes in the history of European imperialism in Africa. This period was marked by intense conflict, profound cultural changes, economic exploitation, and significant social upheaval. The colonization of Algeria had far-reaching impacts on both the Algerian people and French society, and its legacy continues to influence Franco-Algerian relations today.

The conquest of Algeria by France began in 1830 under the pretext of suppressing piracy and reasserting control over the Mediterranean trade routes. However, the underlying motives were more complex, involving the desire to expand French territory, bolster national pride, and divert attention from internal political issues. The initial invasion, led by General de Bourmont, targeted Algiers, the capital of the Ottoman Regency of Algiers. The city fell quickly, and the French established a foothold, but the conquest of the interior regions proved much more challenging and protracted.

The early years of French colonization were characterized by brutal military campaigns aimed at subduing resistance from various Algerian tribes and local leaders. One of the most notable figures of resistance was Emir Abd al-Qadir, who led a protracted and effective guerrilla campaign against the French from 1832 until his capture in 1847. Abd al-Qadir's resistance symbolized the broader Algerian struggle for autonomy and highlighted the resilience and tenacity of the local population in the face of foreign occupation. Despite his eventual defeat, the legacy of his resistance would inspire future generations of Algerian nationalists.

The French employed a strategy of total war, destroying villages, seizing crops, and employing scorched-earth tactics to undermine the support base of the resistance fighters. These tactics caused widespread suffering and displacement among the Algerian population. The French also implemented a policy of land confiscation, seizing fertile lands from indigenous communities and redistributing them to European settlers. This expropriation of land not only disrupted traditional agricultural practices but also entrenched economic inequalities that persisted throughout the colonial period.

The French administration in Algeria evolved over time, moving from military rule to a more structured civil administration. In 1848, Algeria was formally integrated into France as a series of departments, ostensibly making it an integral part of French territory. However, this integration was highly unequal, as the indigenous Algerian population was subjected to discriminatory laws and denied the same rights as European settlers. The French legal system, exemplified by the Code de l'Indigénat, institutionalized these inequalities, subjecting Algerians to a separate and inferior legal status that curtailed their civil liberties and reinforced their subjugation.

Economically, French colonization profoundly transformed Algeria. The introduction of new agricultural practices, the establishment of vineyards, and the development of infrastructure such as railways and ports aimed to integrate Algeria into the French economy and exploit its resources for the benefit of the metropole. The cultivation of cash crops like wine grapes, olives, and citrus fruits flourished, largely controlled by European settlers. This economic model prioritized export-oriented agriculture over subsistence farming, exacerbating food insecurity and contributing to periodic famines among the indigenous population.

Industrial development in Algeria was limited compared to the agricultural sector, but some mining activities, particularly in iron and phosphates, were established. The exploitation of these natural resources further tied Algeria's economy to that of France and reinforced the colonial relationship of dependency. The economic benefits of these developments were largely reaped by the European settlers and French businesses, while the indigenous population remained marginalized and impoverished.

Culturally and socially, French colonization aimed to assimilate Algerians into French civilization, often through coercive and repressive measures. The French educational system was introduced with the intention of promoting French language and culture, but access to education for Algerians was limited and skewed towards creating a small elite loyal to French interests. The vast majority of the indigenous population remained illiterate, with traditional educational institutions such as Qur'anic schools undermined and marginalized.

The French also sought to impose their cultural norms and values, often at the expense of Algerian traditions and Islamic practices. The colonial administration implemented policies that interfered with religious practices, expropriated religious endowments (habous), and attempted to secularize Algerian society. These actions generated significant resentment and resistance among the Algerian population, who saw them as an attack on their identity and way of life.

The social stratification in colonial Algeria was stark, with a clear divide between the European settlers, known as pieds-noirs, and the indigenous Algerians. The pieds-noirs enjoyed political and economic dominance, living in urban areas with modern amenities and benefiting from preferential treatment by the colonial administration. In contrast, the majority of Algerians lived in rural areas or segregated urban quarters, facing systemic discrimination and exploitation.

The tensions and inequalities inherent in the colonial system led to the emergence of a strong nationalist movement in Algeria. The early 20th century saw the formation of various political organizations and movements advocating for Algerian rights and independence. The most prominent among these was the Algerian People's Party (PPA), founded by Messali Hadj in the 1930s. The PPA and other nationalist groups sought to mobilize the Algerian population against colonial rule through political activism, protests, and later armed resistance.

The catalyst for the full-scale struggle for independence came after World War II, as anti-colonial sentiments intensified globally. The brutal suppression of nationalist demonstrations in Setif and Guelma in 1945, which resulted in thousands of Algerian deaths, further fueled the desire for independence. In 1954, the National Liberation Front (FLN) launched an armed insurgency against French rule, marking the beginning of the Algerian War of Independence. The war, which lasted until 1962, was characterized by guerrilla warfare, widespread violence, and atrocities committed by both sides.

The French military response to the FLN insurgency was severe, involving mass arrests, torture, and the use of collective punishment. The conflict also saw significant urban warfare, particularly in Algiers, where the Battle of Algiers (1956-1957) became emblematic of the brutal nature of the struggle. Despite the heavy-handed tactics employed by the French, the FLN managed to sustain its campaign through a combination of military actions, political mobilization, and international diplomacy.

The war had profound effects on French society, causing deep political divisions and leading to a crisis of confidence in the French government. The conflict also sparked widespread debate and controversy within France about the ethics and morality of colonialism, particularly in light of the use of torture and other human rights abuses. The eventual recognition that the war was unwinnable and the mounting pressure from both international and domestic fronts led to negotiations between the French government and the FLN.

In March 1962, the Evian Accords were signed, granting Algeria independence and ending 132 years of French colonial rule. The aftermath of the war was marked by significant upheaval, with large numbers of pieds-noirs and Algerians who had supported the French, known as Harkis, fleeing to France to escape retribution. The newly independent Algeria faced the monumental task of rebuilding a nation ravaged by war and decades of colonial exploitation.

Post-independence, Algeria adopted a socialist-oriented model of development under the leadership of Ahmed Ben Bella and later Houari Boumediene. The government nationalized key industries and resources, seeking to reduce dependency on former colonial powers and address the economic inequalities entrenched by colonial rule. However, the challenges of nation-building, economic development, and social integration proved immense.

The legacy of French colonization in Algeria is deeply complex and multifaceted. It left enduring scars on the Algerian psyche, as well as significant socio-economic and cultural impacts. The period of colonization disrupted traditional social structures, created lasting economic dependencies, and entrenched inequalities that Algeria continues to grapple with. Additionally, the memories of resistance and the struggle for independence have become central to Algerian national identity, shaping contemporary political and social discourse.

For France, the colonization and subsequent war for Algerian independence had profound implications. It forced a reckoning with the ethics and consequences of imperialism, leading to significant political and social changes within France itself. The influx of pieds-noirs and Harkis into France also added new dimensions to French society, contributing to contemporary debates about identity, integration, and the legacy of colonialism.

Chapter 5: Dutch East Indies Control

The Dutch East Indies, now known as Indonesia, were under Dutch colonial control from the early 17th century until the mid-20th century. This period was marked by a complex and often tumultuous history of trade, exploitation, resistance, and significant cultural exchange. The Dutch East Indies played a crucial role in the Dutch global empire, shaping the economic, social, and political landscapes of both Indonesia and the Netherlands.

The origins of Dutch control in the East Indies can be traced back to the early 1600s with the establishment of the Dutch East India Company (VOC). The VOC was a powerful trading company granted a monopoly on Dutch trade in Asia by the Dutch government. It was one of the world's first multinational corporations and wielded immense political and military power. The company's primary goal was to control the lucrative spice trade, which was dominated by the Portuguese and Spanish before the arrival of the Dutch.

The VOC's initial forays into the East Indies were marked by conflict and competition with other European powers and local rulers. The Dutch established their first permanent foothold in the region in 1603 when they captured the Portuguese fort of Ambon in the Moluccas (Spice Islands). This victory was a significant milestone, giving the Dutch control over a key region for spice production. Over the next few decades, the VOC expanded its influence through a combination of military force, strategic alliances, and trade monopolies.

The establishment of Batavia (modern-day Jakarta) in 1619 as the VOC's headquarters marked a pivotal moment in the Dutch colonization of the East Indies. Batavia became the center of Dutch administration and trade in the region, serving as a hub for the collection and distribution of spices and other valuable goods. The city was strategically located on the northwest coast of Java, allowing the

Dutch to control access to the Sunda Strait and dominate maritime trade routes.

The VOC's control over the East Indies was characterized by a ruthless pursuit of profit and a systematic exploitation of the region's resources. The company imposed strict monopolies on the production and trade of spices such as cloves, nutmeg, and mace, often resorting to violent measures to enforce compliance. Local populations were forced into labor, and traditional agricultural practices were disrupted to prioritize the cultivation of cash crops for export.

One of the most notorious episodes of VOC exploitation was the Banda Massacre in 1621. The Dutch sought to secure a monopoly over the nutmeg trade in the Banda Islands, but the local population resisted. In response, the Dutch launched a brutal campaign, killing thousands of Bandanese and forcibly relocating survivors to other islands. This event exemplified the extreme measures the VOC was willing to take to maintain its control and maximize profits.

Despite its wealth and power, the VOC faced numerous challenges in maintaining its dominance in the East Indies. The company's aggressive policies and exploitative practices often led to resistance and rebellion among local populations. Additionally, the VOC had to contend with competition from other European powers, such as the British and French, who sought to establish their own footholds in the region.

In the late 18th century, the VOC began to experience financial difficulties due to corruption, mismanagement, and rising operational costs. The company was also weakened by wars in Europe, which strained Dutch resources and diverted attention away from the colonies. In 1799, the VOC was dissolved, and its assets and territories were taken over by the Dutch government, marking the beginning of direct colonial rule.

The transition from VOC control to Dutch state administration brought about significant changes in the governance and development of the East Indies. The Dutch government implemented reforms aimed at improving efficiency, increasing revenues, and extending control over the archipelago. One of the key figures in this transformation was Governor-General Herman Willem Daendels, who served from 1808 to 1811. Daendels undertook major infrastructure projects, such as the construction of the Great Post Road (De Grote Postweg), which facilitated communication and military movement across Java.

However, the Napoleonic Wars and the subsequent British occupation of Java from 1811 to 1816 temporarily disrupted Dutch control. When the Dutch regained the East Indies following the Treaty of Vienna in 1815, they embarked on a renewed effort to consolidate their authority and exploit the region's resources. This period saw the implementation of the Cultivation System (Cultuurstelsel) in 1830, a coercive agricultural policy that required farmers to dedicate a portion of their land and labor to the cultivation of export crops like coffee, sugar, and indigo.

The Cultivation System had profound social and economic impacts on the East Indies. It generated substantial profits for the Dutch government and contributed significantly to the Dutch economy, financing public works and infrastructure projects in the Netherlands. However, it also led to widespread suffering and exploitation of the indigenous population. Farmers were forced to prioritize cash crops over subsistence agriculture, leading to food shortages and famines. The system entrenched economic inequalities and created a class of wealthy local elites who collaborated with the Dutch administration.

Resistance to Dutch rule continued throughout the 19th century, with numerous uprisings and rebellions challenging colonial authority. One of the most significant of these was the Java War (1825-1830), led by Prince Diponegoro, a Javanese noble who opposed Dutch interference in local affairs. The war was one of the longest and most destructive conflicts in the history of the Dutch East Indies, resulting in significant loss of life and extensive devastation. Although the Dutch eventually emerged victorious, the war underscored the persistent resistance to colonial rule and the difficulties the Dutch faced in maintaining control.

In response to ongoing resistance and changing economic conditions, the Dutch introduced a series of reforms in the late 19th and early 20th centuries. The Ethical Policy, implemented in 1901, aimed to promote the welfare and development of the indigenous population by investing in education, infrastructure, and healthcare. The policy marked a shift from purely exploitative practices to a more paternalistic approach, reflecting broader changes in colonial ideology and the influence of humanitarian and reformist movements in Europe.

Despite these reforms, the fundamental inequalities and exploitative nature of colonial rule persisted. The indigenous population continued to face discrimination and limited political representation. The economic benefits of development were unevenly distributed, with the European and local elites reaping the majority of the rewards. The Ethical Policy also failed to address the underlying grievances and aspirations of the Indonesian people, who increasingly sought greater autonomy and independence.

The early 20th century saw the rise of nationalist movements in the Dutch East Indies, inspired by global anti-colonial struggles and the spread of new political ideologies. Organizations such as Budi Utomo (founded in 1908) and the Indonesian National Party (PNI, founded in 1927) advocated for greater political rights, social reforms, and ultimately independence. The nationalist movement gained momentum in the 1930s, with figures like Sukarno and Mohammad Hatta emerging as prominent leaders.

The outbreak of World War II and the Japanese occupation of the Dutch East Indies from 1942 to 1945 had a profound impact on the trajectory of Indonesian nationalism. The Japanese initially presented themselves as liberators from Dutch colonial rule and promoted

Indonesian nationalism as part of their broader strategy to gain support in occupied territories. While the Japanese occupation was marked by harsh conditions and exploitation, it also disrupted the colonial order and created opportunities for nationalist leaders to mobilize support and gain political experience.

Following Japan's surrender in 1945, Sukarno and Hatta declared Indonesia's independence on August 17, 1945. The declaration was met with immediate resistance from the returning Dutch, leading to a protracted and violent struggle for independence known as the Indonesian National Revolution. The conflict, which lasted until 1949, involved intense military campaigns, guerrilla warfare, and significant civilian suffering. The revolution ended with the Dutch formally recognizing Indonesian independence on December 27, 1949, following international pressure and negotiations mediated by the United Nations.

The legacy of Dutch colonial rule in Indonesia is complex and multifaceted. On one hand, the period of colonization brought about significant economic development, infrastructure improvements, and cultural exchanges. The Dutch introduced new technologies, agricultural practices, and educational institutions that had lasting impacts on Indonesian society. On the other hand, the colonial period was marked by exploitation, oppression, and violence, leaving deep scars on the Indonesian psyche and social fabric.

The economic structures and inequalities established during the colonial period persisted into the post-independence era, shaping Indonesia's development trajectory and contributing to ongoing challenges. The struggle for independence and the experiences of colonialism also played a central role in shaping Indonesian national identity, fostering a sense of unity and resilience among the diverse population.

In contemporary Indonesia, the legacy of Dutch colonial rule is the subject of ongoing reflection and debate. Historical sites, museums, and educational programs seek to preserve and interpret this complex history, acknowledging both the contributions and the injustices of the colonial period. The relationship between Indonesia and the Netherlands has evolved over time, with both countries working to address historical grievances and build a more cooperative and mutually beneficial partnership.

Chapter 6: Portuguese Empire in Brazil

The Portuguese Empire in Brazil, spanning from the early 16th century to the early 19th century, represents one of the most significant and complex episodes in the history of European colonialism in the Americas. This period was marked by the transformation of Brazil from a largely unexplored and sparsely populated region into a crucial part of the Portuguese Empire, characterized by extensive economic exploitation, cultural exchanges, and profound social changes.

The origins of Portuguese interest in Brazil can be traced back to the Treaty of Tordesillas in 1494, which divided the newly discovered lands outside Europe between Portugal and Spain along a meridian 370 leagues west of the Cape Verde islands. Under this treaty, Portugal was entitled to claim territories in the New World to the east of this line. However, it was not until 1500 that the Portuguese explorer Pedro Álvares Cabral officially discovered Brazil. Upon landing on the coast, he claimed the land for Portugal and named it Terra de Vera Cruz, later changed to Brazil due to the valuable brazilwood tree found in the region.

In the early years of Portuguese presence in Brazil, the focus was primarily on the exploitation of brazilwood, a tree that yielded a red dye highly prized in Europe. This trade attracted Portuguese merchants and adventurers, who established trading posts along the coast. However, the Portuguese crown showed little interest in extensive colonization initially, and the territory remained largely unexplored and inhabited by indigenous peoples.

The situation began to change in the 1530s when the Portuguese crown, recognizing the strategic and economic potential of Brazil, decided to implement a more structured and permanent colonization effort. King John III divided the Brazilian territory into fifteen hereditary captaincies, each granted to a nobleman or trusted official who would be responsible for its development and defense. These captaincies were intended to encourage private investment in colonization and to establish a more effective administrative structure. However, the captaincy system faced significant challenges, including resistance from indigenous peoples, hostile European rivals, and internal disputes among the colonists. Many of the captaincies failed to thrive, and the Portuguese crown eventually intervened to centralize control.

The establishment of the Governorate General of Brazil in 1549 marked a turning point in the colonization process. Tomé de Sousa, the first governor-general, founded the city of Salvador in Bahia, which became the capital and administrative center of the colony. Salvador's establishment facilitated more effective governance and coordination of efforts to develop the colony. Under Sousa's leadership, the Portuguese expanded their influence and began to develop the colony's economy.

One of the most significant developments during this period was the introduction of sugarcane cultivation. Sugar quickly became the cornerstone of the Brazilian economy, transforming the colony into one of the world's leading producers of sugar. The establishment of sugar plantations, known as engenhos, required substantial investment in land, labor, and infrastructure. To meet the labor demands of the sugar industry, the Portuguese initially attempted to enslave the indigenous population. However, resistance, high mortality rates, and logistical challenges led to the shift towards African slave labor.

The transatlantic slave trade became integral to the Brazilian economy, with millions of Africans forcibly transported to work on the plantations. The conditions on the plantations were harsh and brutal, with enslaved Africans enduring grueling labor, poor living conditions, and severe punishment. Despite the oppressive conditions, enslaved Africans resisted in various ways, including revolts, escape attempts, and the establishment of quilombos—communities of runaway slaves.

Quilombo dos Palmares, one of the most famous quilombos, was a formidable settlement that resisted Portuguese incursions for decades.

The reliance on slave labor had profound social, economic, and cultural implications for Brazil. It created a rigidly stratified society with a small elite of wealthy plantation owners, a substantial population of enslaved Africans, and a growing mixed-race population resulting from interactions between Europeans, Africans, and indigenous peoples. This complex social structure was characterized by deep inequalities, racial hierarchies, and cultural syncretism.

Throughout the 17th and 18th centuries, Brazil continued to develop economically and socially. The discovery of gold and diamonds in the interior regions of Minas Gerais in the late 17th century spurred a gold rush, attracting thousands of prospectors and settlers. The gold boom brought wealth to the colony and led to the establishment of new towns and infrastructure. However, it also intensified conflicts with indigenous peoples and rival European powers.

The economic prosperity generated by the gold and sugar industries contributed to the growth of urban centers such as Rio de Janeiro, which eventually replaced Salvador as the capital in 1763. Rio de Janeiro's strategic location and growing importance as a port city made it a hub of commerce, culture, and administration. The city's development reflected the broader transformation of Brazil into a more complex and integrated colony within the Portuguese Empire.

The 18th century also saw significant administrative reforms aimed at improving colonial governance and efficiency. The Marquis of Pombal, who served as the de facto ruler of Portugal from 1750 to 1777, implemented a series of reforms that had a lasting impact on Brazil. Pombal sought to strengthen royal authority, promote economic development, and reduce the power of the Catholic Church and local elites. His reforms included the expulsion of the Jesuits, who had significant influence in the colony, the reorganization of the colonial administration, and the promotion of education and economic diversification.

Despite these efforts, tensions and conflicts persisted in the colony. The heavy taxation and exploitation imposed by the Portuguese crown led to widespread discontent among the colonists. The Inconfidência Mineira, a conspiracy led by a group of Brazilian intellectuals and military officers in Minas Gerais in 1789, was one of the most notable expressions of this discontent. Inspired by Enlightenment ideals and the American and French revolutions, the conspirators sought to establish an independent republic. However, the plot was discovered, and its leaders, including the famous Tiradentes, were arrested and executed.

The early 19th century brought significant changes to Brazil and the Portuguese Empire. The Napoleonic Wars in Europe had a profound impact on Portugal, leading to the transfer of the Portuguese royal court to Brazil in 1808. King John VI and his court established themselves in Rio de Janeiro, transforming the city into the de facto capital of the Portuguese Empire. This relocation had far-reaching implications, elevating Brazil's status within the empire and stimulating economic and cultural development.

The presence of the royal court in Brazil brought new opportunities and challenges. It facilitated closer ties between Brazil and Portugal, encouraged investment in infrastructure and industry, and promoted cultural and intellectual exchange. The establishment of institutions such as the Royal Library, the Botanical Garden, and the Military Academy contributed to the colony's development and modernization.

However, the royal court's presence also exacerbated existing social and political tensions. The lavish lifestyle of the court contrasted sharply with the poverty and exploitation experienced by many Brazilians. The influx of Portuguese officials and merchants fueled resentment among the local population, who felt marginalized and excluded from power. These tensions were further aggravated by the economic hardships caused by the Napoleonic Wars and subsequent political instability in Europe.

The political landscape in Brazil began to shift dramatically in the early 1820s. Inspired by the wave of independence movements sweeping across Latin America, Brazilian nationalists and reformers increasingly called for greater autonomy and self-governance. The return of King John VI to Portugal in 1821 left his son, Pedro, as regent of Brazil. In response to growing demands for independence, Pedro declared Brazil's independence from Portugal on September 7, 1822, becoming Emperor Pedro I of Brazil.

The declaration of independence marked the beginning of a new chapter in Brazilian history. The transition from a colony to an independent nation was fraught with challenges, including internal conflicts, economic difficulties, and the need to establish a stable political system. The early years of independence were marked by struggles between different factions, including monarchists, republicans, and regional leaders vying for power.

Despite these challenges, Brazil emerged as a sovereign nation with a unique identity shaped by its colonial past. The legacy of Portuguese rule had a profound impact on Brazilian society, culture, and institutions. The Portuguese language, Roman Catholicism, and legal and administrative systems left an enduring imprint on the nation. The complex social hierarchies and racial dynamics established during the colonial period continued to influence Brazilian society, contributing to ongoing struggles for equality and social justice.

Chapter 7: Belgian Exploitation of the Congo

The Belgian exploitation of the Congo stands as one of the most harrowing and significant episodes in the history of colonialism, revealing the extremes of imperial greed, brutality, and the catastrophic impacts on indigenous populations. This period, spanning from the late 19th century until the mid-20th century, is marked by the establishment and rule of the Congo Free State by King Leopold II of Belgium and the subsequent Belgian colonial administration. The history of Belgian control over the Congo can be divided into two distinct phases: the Congo Free State (1885-1908) and the Belgian Congo (1908-1960).

The origins of Belgian interest in the Congo can be traced back to the ambitions of King Leopold II, who harbored imperial aspirations and sought to enhance Belgium's stature on the global stage through colonial expansion. Unlike other European powers, Belgium did not possess a significant colonial empire, which fueled Leopold's determination to acquire territories overseas. His focus turned towards the largely unexplored and resource-rich region of Central Africa, particularly the Congo River Basin.

Leopold initially presented his colonial ambitions under the guise of humanitarian and scientific exploration. In 1876, he organized the International African Association, ostensibly to promote the exploration and civilization of Central Africa. This association later evolved into the International Association of the Congo, a private enterprise through which Leopold aimed to establish control over the region. He employed the famous explorer Henry Morton Stanley to secure treaties with local African chiefs, often through deceit and coercion, thereby gaining control over vast territories.

In 1885, at the Berlin Conference, European powers formally recognized Leopold's claims to the Congo, and the Congo Free State was established under his personal rule. This vast territory, approximately 76 times the size of Belgium, was essentially Leopold's private property, distinct from the Belgian state. Leopold presented the Congo Free State as a philanthropic endeavor, committed to abolishing the Arab slave trade, promoting Christianity, and bringing civilization to the indigenous peoples. However, the reality was starkly different.

Leopold's primary motive was to extract wealth from the Congo, and he established an exploitative economic system to achieve this. The Congo Free State became infamous for its brutal extraction of rubber, ivory, and other resources. Rubber, in particular, became highly lucrative due to the growing demand for rubber in industrialized nations. The methods used to extract these resources were characterized by extreme violence and coercion. Indigenous people were forced into labor, and failure to meet quotas often resulted in horrific punishments, including mutilation, flogging, and execution.

The Force Publique, a paramilitary force composed of African soldiers and European officers, enforced Leopold's regime through terror and violence. Villages were raided, women and children were taken hostage to ensure men met rubber quotas, and punitive expeditions were conducted to suppress resistance. The systematic brutality led to widespread depopulation and suffering. Estimates suggest that millions of Congolese died as a direct result of the exploitation, forced labor, disease, and famine during Leopold's rule.

The atrocities committed in the Congo eventually attracted international condemnation. Missionaries, former officials, and journalists, notably E.D. Morel and Roger Casement, exposed the horrific conditions and human rights abuses. The Congo Reform Association, founded by Morel and others, played a crucial role in raising awareness and pressuring the international community to act. Their efforts culminated in widespread outrage and calls for reform.

In 1908, under mounting international pressure and financial difficulties, King Leopold II was forced to cede control of the Congo Free State to the Belgian government. The territory was renamed the Belgian Congo, and it became a colony under direct Belgian administration. While the transition marked the end of Leopold's personal rule, the exploitation and suffering of the Congolese people did not cease entirely.

Under Belgian colonial rule, the economic exploitation of the Congo continued, albeit with some administrative and infrastructural improvements. The Belgian administration invested in railways, roads, and healthcare, and educational facilities, but these developments primarily served the interests of the colonial economy and European settlers rather than the welfare of the Congolese population. The colony remained a major source of raw materials, including rubber, copper, and other minerals, which were exported to fuel Belgium's industrial growth.

The Belgian colonial system was paternalistic and deeply racist. The administration imposed a strict social hierarchy, with Europeans at the top, a small class of educated Congolese known as évolués below them, and the vast majority of the indigenous population at the bottom. The évolués, who were educated in mission schools and often employed in lower-level administrative roles, faced significant discrimination and were denied political rights. The Belgian authorities maintained tight control over political activities and suppressed nationalist movements.

The imposition of European culture and values was central to Belgian colonial policy. Missionary education aimed to assimilate the Congolese into European ways of thinking and living, often at the expense of indigenous cultures and traditions. Traditional institutions and leadership structures were undermined or co-opted to serve colonial interests. The Congolese were subjected to harsh labor conditions, heavy taxation, and land expropriation, which disrupted their traditional livelihoods and communities.

Despite these oppressive conditions, the early 20th century saw the emergence of Congolese resistance and nationalist movements. World War II played a significant role in shaping these movements, as many Congolese soldiers who served in the war returned with heightened political awareness and aspirations for independence. The post-war period saw increased political activity and the formation of political parties and associations advocating for Congolese rights and self-determination.

The momentum for independence grew throughout the 1950s, fueled by global decolonization trends and internal pressures. The Belgian government, facing growing unrest and international scrutiny, began to make concessions. In 1959, widespread riots in the capital city of Léopoldville (now Kinshasa) and other major cities underscored the urgent demand for independence. In response, Belgium announced a rapid transition plan, leading to the independence of the Congo on June 30, 1960.

The transition to independence was tumultuous and fraught with challenges. The newly independent Democratic Republic of the Congo, led by Prime Minister Patrice Lumumba, faced immediate political instability, regional secessionist movements, and external interference, particularly from Cold War superpowers. The assassination of Lumumba and the subsequent rise of Mobutu Sese Seko's dictatorial regime marked the beginning of a long period of political turmoil and economic decline.

The legacy of Belgian colonialism in the Congo is complex and enduring. The extraction of wealth and resources left a deep economic imbalance, and the artificial borders drawn by colonial powers contributed to ongoing ethnic and regional conflicts. The suppression of political development and education under Belgian rule left the newly independent nation with weak institutions and limited human capital to manage its affairs.

In contemporary times, the Democratic Republic of the Congo continues to grapple with the consequences of its colonial past. The country's vast natural resources, including minerals critical to modern technology, remain a source of both potential wealth and ongoing conflict. Efforts to address the legacies of exploitation and underdevelopment are ongoing, with a focus on promoting sustainable development, political stability, and human rights.

The Belgian exploitation of the Congo serves as a stark reminder of the profound and often devastating impacts of colonialism. It highlights the complexities of imperialism, the brutal realities of economic exploitation, and the enduring challenges faced by post-colonial societies. Understanding this history is crucial for acknowledging the suffering endured by the Congolese people and for fostering a more just and equitable future.

Chapter 8: Italian Colonialism in Libya

Italian colonialism in Libya represents a significant and complex chapter in the history of North Africa and the broader history of European imperialism. This period, spanning from 1911 to 1943, encompasses the initial invasion and conquest, the establishment of colonial rule, the impact of fascism under Mussolini, and the eventual downfall during World War II. The legacy of Italian rule in Libya has left deep scars and enduring influences on the country's socio-political landscape.

The story of Italian colonial ambitions in Libya begins in the late 19th and early 20th centuries. Italy, a relatively latecomer to the scramble for African colonies compared to other European powers, sought to assert its presence on the global stage and compete with established colonial empires. By the early 20th century, the Kingdom of Italy, under the monarchy and influenced by nationalist and expansionist sentiments, targeted the Ottoman-controlled territories of Tripolitania, Cyrenaica, and Fezzan, collectively known as Libya.

The Italo-Turkish War of 1911-1912 marked the beginning of Italian efforts to seize control of Libya. The war was prompted by Italy's desire to exploit the strategic location and potential resources of the region. In September 1911, Italy launched a series of naval and amphibious attacks on key coastal cities, including Tripoli and Benghazi. The Italian military campaign was initially successful in capturing these coastal areas, but the subsequent guerilla resistance by local Libyan tribes, particularly the Senussi Order in Cyrenaica, prolonged the conflict and revealed the challenges of subjugating the interior regions.

The Treaty of Ouchy (also known as the Treaty of Lausanne) in October 1912 formally ended the Italo-Turkish War, with the Ottoman Empire ceding its claims to Libya to Italy. Despite this nominal victory, Italian control over Libya remained tenuous and largely confined to coastal cities. The resistance of Libyan tribes, motivated by both anti-colonial sentiment and religious fervor, continued to pose a significant obstacle to Italian consolidation of power.

The early years of Italian colonial rule in Libya were marked by a combination of military campaigns and attempts to establish administrative control. The Italians faced fierce resistance from various tribal groups, particularly in the interior regions of Cyrenaica and Fezzan. The Senussi Order, a Sufi brotherhood with significant influence in Cyrenaica, played a central role in organizing and sustaining the resistance. The charismatic leadership of figures such as Omar Mukhtar galvanized the Libyan resistance movement, leading to protracted guerrilla warfare against Italian forces.

The 1920s and 1930s saw intensified efforts by Italy to pacify and control Libya. The rise of Benito Mussolini and the establishment of the Fascist regime in Italy in 1922 had a profound impact on the colonial policy in Libya. Mussolini's government sought to assert Italian dominance and integrate Libya more fully into the Italian state. This period was characterized by a brutal and systematic campaign to suppress resistance and establish firm colonial rule.

One of the most notorious aspects of Italian colonial rule in Libya was the implementation of a policy of forced displacement and concentration camps. To break the back of the resistance, the Italian military, under commanders such as General Rodolfo Graziani, resorted to ruthless tactics, including the destruction of villages, the confiscation of livestock, and the internment of thousands of Libyans in concentration camps. These camps, located in harsh desert areas, were designed to isolate and demoralize the population. The conditions in the camps were appalling, with inadequate food, water, and medical care, leading to high mortality rates. The most infamous of these camps was in the town of El Agheila.

The resistance leader Omar Mukhtar, known as the "Lion of the Desert," became a symbol of Libyan defiance. His capture in 1931 marked a significant turning point in the Italian campaign. Mukhtar was subjected to a show trial and publicly executed, further intensifying the repression but also solidifying his status as a national hero and martyr in the eyes of many Libyans.

Despite the harsh measures, the Italian regime also sought to portray itself as a modernizing force in Libya. The Fascist government initiated various infrastructure projects, including the construction of roads, railways, and public buildings, aimed at integrating Libya into the Italian economy and demonstrating the benefits of colonial rule. The regime promoted Italian settlement in Libya, encouraging Italian farmers to emigrate and establish agricultural colonies. This policy, however, often involved the expropriation of fertile lands from Libyan peasants, exacerbating local grievances.

The demographic and economic policies of the Italian regime had mixed results. While some urban areas saw development and modernization, the benefits were unevenly distributed, and the majority of the Libyan population remained marginalized. The introduction of Italian legal and educational systems sought to assimilate Libyans into the colonial framework, but these efforts often clashed with indigenous customs and traditions, leading to cultural tensions.

The outbreak of World War II in 1939 brought significant changes to the colonial landscape in Libya. The strategic importance of Libya as a base for military operations in North Africa drew the attention of both the Axis and Allied powers. Libya became a major battleground during the North African campaign, with significant battles such as those at El Alamein and Tobruk.

The war had a profound impact on the Italian colonial administration in Libya. The initial successes of the Axis forces, including the German Afrika Korps led by General Erwin Rommel, were followed by eventual defeats at the hands of the Allied forces. By 1943, the Allied victory in North Africa led to the collapse of Italian control over Libya. The retreating Italian and German forces left behind a devastated landscape and a population that had endured years of hardship and conflict.

The defeat of the Axis powers and the subsequent occupation of Libya by Allied forces marked the end of Italian colonial rule. In the post-war period, Libya was placed under British and French military administration, paving the way for the eventual establishment of an independent Libyan state. The legacy of Italian colonialism, however, continued to shape the country's socio-political landscape.

The period of Italian rule left deep scars on Libyan society. The policies of forced displacement, economic exploitation, and cultural assimilation had long-lasting effects on the population. The infrastructure projects initiated by the Italians, while contributing to modernization, also reinforced patterns of inequality and economic dependency. The memory of resistance leaders like Omar Mukhtar and the collective experience of suffering under colonial rule became central to Libyan national identity.

In the post-colonial period, Libya underwent significant political changes, culminating in the rise of Muammar Gaddafi in 1969. Gaddafi's regime sought to redefine Libyan identity and position the country as a leader of anti-colonial and anti-imperialist movements. The legacy of Italian colonialism was often invoked in political discourse to emphasize the importance of sovereignty and resistance against foreign domination.

The relationship between Libya and Italy also evolved in the post-colonial era. Efforts at reconciliation included economic cooperation, compensation for colonial-era injustices, and cultural exchanges. However, the legacy of colonialism continued to influence bilateral relations, with periodic tensions and disputes over issues such as migration and historical memory.

In contemporary Libya, the impact of Italian colonialism remains a subject of historical inquiry and political reflection. The period of Italian rule is remembered both for its brutality and for its attempts at modernization. The experience of resistance and resilience during the colonial era continues to inspire national pride and informs the ongoing struggle for political stability and development.

Italian colonialism in Libya thus represents a complex and multifaceted chapter in the history of both nations. It highlights the dynamics of imperial ambition, resistance, and the enduring legacies of colonial rule. Understanding this history is crucial for appreciating the contemporary challenges faced by Libya and for fostering a more nuanced and informed dialogue about the colonial past.

Chapter 9: German Empire in Namibia

The German Empire in Namibia, formerly known as German South West Africa, represents one of the darkest chapters in the history of colonialism and imperialism. This period, spanning from the late 19th century until the early 20th century, is marked by the brutal subjugation of indigenous populations, economic exploitation, and one of the first genocides of the 20th century. The legacy of German colonial rule in Namibia continues to resonate in the country's social, political, and economic landscape.

The origins of German colonial ambitions in Namibia can be traced back to the late 19th century, during the height of the European scramble for Africa. Germany, having unified in 1871 under Otto von Bismarck, sought to assert itself as a major imperial power alongside Britain, France, and other European nations. Namibia, with its vast arid landscapes and strategic location, attracted German interest as a potential colony.

The formal establishment of German colonial rule in Namibia began in 1884 when the German trader Adolf Lüderitz acquired land from indigenous leaders under dubious circumstances. Lüderitz's acquisitions were subsequently backed by the German government, which declared the region a protectorate. This marked the beginning of German South West Africa, the first German colony in Africa. The initial period of German rule involved the establishment of administrative structures, military outposts, and settlements by German colonists.

German colonial rule in Namibia was characterized by a rigid and hierarchical administrative system. The colonial government, headquartered in Windhoek, was headed by a governor who wielded considerable authority over both the European settlers and the indigenous population. The German administration sought to impose European legal, economic, and social systems on the colony, often disregarding and undermining traditional African governance structures and cultural practices.

The German colonial economy in Namibia was primarily extractive, focusing on the exploitation of the colony's natural resources. The discovery of minerals, particularly diamonds, in the early 20th century further intensified German economic interests in the region. German settlers and companies established large farms and mining enterprises, often expropriating land from indigenous communities. The introduction of forced labor policies subjected the local population to harsh working conditions in mines, farms, and infrastructure projects, fueling resentment and resistance.

The imposition of German colonial rule met with significant resistance from the indigenous communities, particularly the Herero and Nama peoples. The tensions between the colonizers and the indigenous populations eventually culminated in one of the most tragic episodes of colonial history: the Herero and Namaqua genocide. In 1904, the Herero people, led by Chief Samuel Maharero, rose in rebellion against the German authorities, driven by grievances over land expropriation, forced labor, and oppressive policies. The Nama people, under the leadership of Hendrik Witbooi, also joined the uprising.

The German response to the uprising was brutal and ruthless. The colonial administration, under the command of General Lothar von Trotha, launched a campaign of extermination against the Herero and Nama. Von Trotha issued the infamous Vernichtungsbefehl, or extermination order, which aimed to annihilate the Herero people. The German military forces attacked Herero villages, killing men, women, and children, and driving survivors into the harsh Kalahari Desert, where many perished from starvation and dehydration. The Nama faced similar atrocities, with their population subjected to massacres, forced relocations, and internment in concentration camps.

The genocide resulted in the deaths of an estimated 80% of the Herero population and 50% of the Nama population. The survivors were subjected to severe repression, including internment in concentration camps such as Shark Island, where they faced inhumane conditions, forced labor, and medical experiments. The events of 1904-1908 left a lasting scar on the indigenous communities, decimating their populations and disrupting their social structures.

Following the genocide, German colonial rule in Namibia continued with a focus on consolidating control and furthering economic exploitation. The colonial administration implemented policies aimed at integrating the colony into the German Empire's economic framework. Infrastructure projects, such as railways and ports, were developed to facilitate the extraction and export of resources. German settlers continued to establish farms and businesses, often benefiting from preferential treatment by the colonial authorities.

The outbreak of World War I in 1914 brought significant changes to German colonial rule in Namibia. The colony became a battleground between German forces and the South African troops of the British Empire. In 1915, German South West Africa was captured by South African forces, and the colony was placed under South African administration. The Treaty of Versailles in 1919 officially transferred control of the territory from Germany to South Africa, marking the end of German colonial rule.

The legacy of German colonialism in Namibia is multifaceted and enduring. The genocide of the Herero and Nama peoples stands as a stark reminder of the atrocities committed during the colonial period. The forced labor, land expropriation, and economic exploitation left deep scars on the indigenous communities, contributing to long-term socio-economic disparities and grievances. The imposition of European legal and administrative systems disrupted traditional governance structures, leading to lasting cultural and social impacts.

In the post-colonial period, Namibia's struggle for independence from South African rule, which was itself characterized by apartheid policies, further shaped the country's trajectory. The memory of German colonial atrocities played a significant role in the national consciousness and the anti-colonial liberation movement. Namibia finally achieved independence in 1990, following a protracted armed struggle led by the South West Africa People's Organization (SWAPO).

The independent Namibian government has sought to address the historical injustices and legacy of colonialism through various measures. Land reform policies aim to redistribute land to historically marginalized communities, although this process has faced challenges and controversies. Efforts to commemorate and honor the victims of the Herero and Nama genocide include the construction of memorials, the return of ancestral remains from Germany, and ongoing calls for reparations and formal apologies from the German government.

In recent years, the relationship between Namibia and Germany has been shaped by efforts to reconcile and address the colonial past. In 2021, the German government formally recognized the genocide and offered a financial compensation package to support development projects in affected communities. While this move was a significant step towards reconciliation, it also sparked debates about the adequacy and appropriateness of the measures, with some critics arguing that the compensation fell short of addressing the full extent of the historical injustices.

The legacy of German colonialism in Namibia continues to influence the country's socio-political landscape. The historical grievances and socio-economic disparities rooted in the colonial period remain pressing issues. The process of reconciliation and addressing historical injustices is ongoing, reflecting the complexities of dealing with a traumatic and contentious past. Understanding the history of German colonialism in Namibia is crucial for appreciating the contemporary challenges and dynamics within the country and for fostering a more just and equitable future.

The German Empire's rule in Namibia serves as a stark example of the brutalities and injustices of colonialism. The genocide of the Herero and Nama peoples, the economic exploitation, and the cultural disruptions inflicted by German colonial policies have left an indelible mark on Namibia's history. The ongoing efforts to address and reconcile with this past underscore the importance of acknowledging and learning from historical injustices in the pursuit of a more just and inclusive society.

Chapter 10: British Rule in America

British rule in America, which spanned from the early 17th century to the late 18th century, represents a significant period in the history of both Britain and what would eventually become the United States. This era is characterized by the establishment of colonies, the development of economic systems, cultural exchanges, conflicts with Indigenous peoples, and ultimately the struggle for independence. The legacy of British colonial rule in America has had a lasting impact on the political, social, and cultural landscape of the United States.

The origins of British colonial ambitions in America can be traced back to the late 16th and early 17th centuries. Driven by a combination of economic interests, religious motivations, and national rivalry with other European powers, England sought to establish a foothold in the New World. The earliest attempts at colonization, such as the ill-fated Roanoke Colony in the 1580s, ended in failure. However, the successful establishment of Jamestown in 1607 marked the beginning of permanent British settlements in North America.

Jamestown, located in present-day Virginia, was founded by the Virginia Company, a joint-stock company seeking to profit from the resources of the New World. The early years of the colony were marked by severe hardships, including disease, starvation, and conflicts with the Indigenous Powhatan Confederacy. Despite these challenges, the colony eventually stabilized and grew, largely due to the cultivation of tobacco, which became a highly profitable cash crop.

The success of Jamestown spurred further British colonization efforts along the Atlantic coast. Throughout the 17th century, a series of colonies were established, each with its unique characteristics and motivations. The New England colonies, such as Plymouth (1620) and Massachusetts Bay (1630), were founded primarily by Puritans seeking religious freedom and the opportunity to build a "city upon a hill" that would serve as a model Christian society. These colonies developed a relatively egalitarian social structure, with a focus on community and religious observance.

In contrast, the Middle Colonies, including New York, New Jersey, Pennsylvania, and Delaware, were more diverse in terms of both population and economy. Pennsylvania, founded by William Penn in 1681, became known for its religious tolerance and democratic principles. The economy of the Middle Colonies was a mix of agriculture, commerce, and manufacturing, benefiting from fertile land and navigable rivers.

The Southern Colonies, which included Maryland, Virginia, the Carolinas, and Georgia, developed economies based on plantation agriculture. These colonies relied heavily on the labor of enslaved Africans to cultivate cash crops such as tobacco, rice, and indigo. The institution of slavery became deeply entrenched in the Southern colonies, shaping their social and economic structures.

The colonial period was marked by significant interactions and conflicts with Indigenous peoples. British settlers often encroached on Native American lands, leading to a series of wars and skirmishes. Some Indigenous groups, such as the Iroquois Confederacy, engaged in complex alliances and trade relationships with the British, while others, such as the Powhatan and Pequot, experienced violent conflicts and displacement.

The economic policies of the British government played a crucial role in shaping the colonial economy. The Navigation Acts, beginning in 1651, were a series of laws designed to ensure that the economic benefits of colonial trade flowed back to Britain. These acts restricted the colonies' trade with other nations and required that certain goods be shipped only in British vessels. While these policies were intended to strengthen the British economy, they often led to resentment and smuggling in the colonies.

The relationship between the colonies and the British government became increasingly strained in the 18th century. The Seven Years'

War (1756-1763), known in America as the French and Indian War, was a pivotal conflict that pitted British and colonial forces against the French and their Native American allies. The war ended with a British victory and the acquisition of vast territories in North America. However, the financial cost of the war led the British government to seek new sources of revenue from the colonies.

In the aftermath of the war, the British government implemented a series of taxes and regulations aimed at increasing revenue from the colonies. The Stamp Act of 1765, which imposed a tax on printed materials, and the Townshend Acts of 1767, which placed duties on imported goods, were particularly unpopular. These measures were seen by many colonists as violations of their rights as Englishmen, particularly the principle of "no taxation without representation."

The growing discontent in the colonies gave rise to a movement for greater autonomy and resistance to British rule. The formation of groups such as the Sons of Liberty, the organization of colonial assemblies, and widespread protests and boycotts demonstrated the increasing unity and resolve of the colonists. The Boston Massacre in 1770 and the Boston Tea Party in 1773 were significant events that further inflamed tensions.

The situation reached a breaking point in 1774 with the passage of the Coercive Acts, also known as the Intolerable Acts, which were designed to punish Massachusetts for the Boston Tea Party. These acts, which included the closing of Boston Harbor and the revocation of Massachusetts' charter, galvanized colonial opposition and led to the convening of the First Continental Congress. This body of delegates from the colonies sought to coordinate a response to British policies and assert their rights.

The outbreak of armed conflict between British troops and colonial militias at Lexington and Concord in April 1775 marked the beginning of the American Revolutionary War. The war, which lasted until 1783, was a protracted and bloody struggle that saw significant battles such as Bunker Hill, Saratoga, and Yorktown. The leadership of figures such as George Washington, the support of foreign allies like France, and the resilience and determination of the colonial forces were key factors in securing victory.

The Declaration of Independence, adopted by the Continental Congress on July 4, 1776, formally asserted the colonies' intention to separate from Britain and establish themselves as an independent nation. The document, primarily authored by Thomas Jefferson, articulated the philosophical justifications for independence, emphasizing the principles of natural rights and the social contract.

The Treaty of Paris, signed in 1783, officially ended the war and recognized the independence of the United States. The new nation faced the daunting task of creating a stable and effective government. The Articles of Confederation, adopted during the war, proved inadequate in providing a strong central authority. This led to the Constitutional Convention of 1787, where the current Constitution of the United States was drafted and subsequently ratified.

The legacy of British rule in America is multifaceted. On one hand, the colonial period established foundational political, legal, and cultural traditions that continue to influence American society. The British legal system, principles of representative government, and cultural practices left an indelible mark on the emerging American identity. On the other hand, the period of British rule also left deep scars, particularly in terms of the treatment of Indigenous peoples and the institution of slavery.

The struggle for independence and the subsequent formation of the United States had profound global implications. The American Revolution inspired other movements for independence and democratic governance, particularly in Europe and Latin America. The ideals of liberty and self-determination articulated during the Revolution continue to resonate and shape political discourse worldwide.

In contemporary America, the legacy of British colonial rule is remembered and interpreted in various ways. The revolutionary struggle is celebrated as a foundational moment in the nation's history, symbolizing the triumph of liberty and justice. However, there is also a growing recognition of the complexities and contradictions of this period, including the experiences of marginalized groups and the impact of colonial policies on Indigenous populations.

British rule in America represents a significant and transformative era that laid the groundwork for the birth of a new nation. The colonization process, economic development, cultural exchanges, and the eventual struggle for independence are integral to understanding the historical trajectory of the United States. The enduring legacy of this period continues to shape the nation's identity, values, and aspirations, underscoring the importance of historical reflection and critical examination.

Chapter 11: Japanese Occupation of Korea

The Japanese occupation of Korea, which lasted from 1910 to 1945, is a deeply significant and complex period in the history of Korea and East Asia. This era was marked by Japan's efforts to assimilate Korea into its empire, leading to profound changes in Korean society, economy, and culture. The occupation had lasting repercussions, contributing to Korea's eventual division and shaping its post-World War II trajectory.

The roots of the Japanese occupation of Korea can be traced back to the late 19th century, a period of significant upheaval and transformation in East Asia. The decline of the Qing Dynasty in China, the rise of Japan as a regional power, and the geopolitical interests of Western imperial powers created a volatile environment. Japan, having undergone the Meiji Restoration in 1868, was rapidly modernizing and seeking to expand its influence in the region.

The initial stages of Japanese interest in Korea were marked by diplomatic and military maneuvers. The Treaty of Ganghwa in 1876, imposed by Japan, forced Korea to open its ports to Japanese trade, signaling the beginning of Japan's encroachment on Korean sovereignty. The ensuing years saw Japan's influence in Korea grow, often at the expense of Chinese and Russian interests. The First Sino-Japanese War (1894-1895) and the Russo-Japanese War (1904-1905) were pivotal conflicts that solidified Japan's dominance in Korea. The Treaty of Shimonoseki, which ended the Sino-Japanese War, and the Treaty of Portsmouth, which concluded the Russo-Japanese War, both acknowledged Japan's interests in Korea.

In 1905, Japan established a protectorate over Korea through the Eulsa Treaty, which was signed under duress and is widely considered illegitimate by Koreans. This treaty stripped Korea of its diplomatic sovereignty, placing its foreign affairs under Japanese control. The final step in Japan's annexation of Korea came in 1910, when the Japan-Korea Annexation Treaty was signed, again under coercive circumstances. This treaty formally annexed Korea into the Japanese Empire, marking the beginning of 35 years of colonial rule.

The Japanese occupation was characterized by efforts to integrate Korea into the Japanese Empire through a combination of political control, economic exploitation, and cultural assimilation. The Japanese colonial administration, headed by a Governor-General, exercised autocratic control over Korea. Korean political institutions were dismantled, and Japanese officials occupied key positions in government, law enforcement, and the military. The administration implemented a series of policies aimed at modernizing Korea's infrastructure, economy, and educational system, but these initiatives were primarily designed to benefit Japan.

Economic exploitation was a central feature of Japanese rule. Korea's agricultural sector was restructured to serve Japanese needs, with rice and other crops being exported to Japan. Land ownership patterns were altered through land surveys and reallocation, often disadvantaging Korean farmers. Industrial development was promoted, particularly in sectors that supported Japan's war efforts, such as mining and heavy industry. Korean labor was mobilized to support these industries, often under harsh conditions. The economic policies of the colonial administration led to significant social and economic changes in Korea, including urbanization and the growth of a working-class population.

Cultural assimilation, or "Japanization," was another key aspect of the occupation. The Japanese government sought to suppress Korean identity and promote Japanese culture and language. Korean schools were required to teach in Japanese, and the use of the Korean language was discouraged in public life. Korean history and culture were marginalized in favor of Japanese history and values. Traditional

Korean customs and practices were often suppressed, and Koreans were encouraged, and later forced, to adopt Japanese names. Shinto shrines were established throughout Korea, and Koreans were pressured to participate in Shinto rituals.

Resistance to Japanese rule took many forms, ranging from passive resistance and cultural preservation efforts to active, organized resistance movements. One of the most significant acts of resistance was the March 1st Movement in 1919, a nationwide protest that called for Korean independence. Inspired by the principles of self-determination outlined in U.S. President Woodrow Wilson's Fourteen Points and the global wave of decolonization, the movement saw widespread participation from various segments of Korean society, including students, intellectuals, and religious leaders. The Japanese response to the March 1st Movement was brutal, with thousands of Koreans being arrested, and many were killed or injured. Despite the suppression, the movement galvanized Korean nationalism and highlighted the desire for independence.

Throughout the occupation, numerous underground organizations and exile groups worked towards Korean independence. The Provisional Government of the Republic of Korea, established in Shanghai in 1919, played a central role in coordinating resistance efforts. Korean independence activists, such as Kim Gu, Syngman Rhee, and An Jung-geun, carried out diplomatic, military, and political campaigns to garner international support and challenge Japanese rule. These efforts included armed resistance, propaganda activities, and diplomatic outreach to countries like the United States and China.

The occupation also had profound social and cultural impacts on Korean society. The policies of assimilation and repression led to significant changes in Korean identity and culture. While some Koreans collaborated with the Japanese administration, many others sought to preserve their cultural heritage through clandestine education and cultural activities. The period saw the emergence of new cultural movements, such as the Korean Renaissance, which sought to blend traditional Korean elements with modern influences. Literature, art, and theater became important mediums for expressing Korean identity and resistance.

World War II marked a turning point in the Japanese occupation of Korea. As Japan's war effort intensified, the demands on Korea increased. Koreans were conscripted into the Japanese military and forced into labor to support the war. The exploitation reached its peak with the establishment of "comfort stations," where Korean women were coerced into sexual slavery for Japanese soldiers. The suffering and exploitation during this period left deep scars on Korean society.

The end of World War II in 1945 brought about the collapse of the Japanese Empire and the liberation of Korea. However, the legacy of Japanese rule continued to affect Korea's post-war development. The abrupt departure of Japanese officials left a power vacuum, contributing to political instability and the eventual division of Korea into two separate states: North Korea and South Korea. The division, which was initially intended as a temporary measure by the Allied powers, became permanent due to Cold War rivalries, leading to the Korean War and ongoing tensions on the Korean Peninsula.

The occupation period has had a lasting impact on Korean society, politics, and culture. The experiences of colonization and resistance have shaped Korean national identity and continue to influence contemporary issues, such as historical memory and reconciliation with Japan. The legacy of Japanese rule is a contentious topic in Korea-Japan relations, with disputes over issues like wartime reparations, the treatment of "comfort women," and historical interpretation remaining unresolved.

In modern Korea, the memory of the occupation is preserved through various means, including education, memorials, and cultural works. Museums and historical sites dedicated to the period serve as reminders of the struggles and resilience of the Korean people. The experiences of the occupation have been depicted in literature, film, and art, contributing to a collective understanding of this pivotal period in Korean history.

The Japanese occupation of Korea was a period of profound change and suffering for the Korean people. The policies of political control, economic exploitation, and cultural assimilation had lasting effects on Korean society, contributing to the development of a strong national identity and a deep-seated desire for independence. The legacy of the occupation continues to shape Korea's relationship with Japan and its own national consciousness, underscoring the importance of historical memory and the ongoing quest for justice and reconciliation.

Chapter 12: British Colonialism in Australia

British colonialism in Australia, which began with the arrival of the First Fleet in 1788 and extended well into the 20th century, is a multifaceted and complex chapter in both British and Australian history. This era is characterized by the establishment and expansion of European settlements, the impact on Indigenous populations, the development of colonial economies and societies, and the eventual emergence of Australia as a nation. The colonization process involved a mix of strategic considerations, economic interests, and social dynamics, all of which contributed to the profound transformation of the continent.

The arrival of the First Fleet in Botany Bay in January 1788 marked the beginning of British settlement in Australia. Under the command of Captain Arthur Phillip, the fleet consisted of 11 ships carrying over 1,400 people, including convicts, marines, and officials. The decision to establish a penal colony in Australia was influenced by multiple factors, including the need to alleviate overcrowded British prisons, the desire to assert British presence in the Pacific, and the strategic importance of securing a foothold in the region. The initial settlement was moved to Port Jackson, now known as Sydney, where better resources and natural harbors were found.

The early years of the colony were marked by significant challenges, including harsh environmental conditions, food shortages, and conflicts with the Indigenous populations. The British settlers were largely unprepared for the Australian environment, and the initial years were a struggle for survival. However, through perseverance and adaptation, the colony gradually became more self-sufficient. Agriculture, initially focused on subsistence farming, began to expand, and sheep farming emerged as a significant industry due to the suitability of the Australian landscape for wool production. The introduction of sheep by John Macarthur in the early 19th century laid the foundation for the wool industry, which would become a cornerstone of the colonial economy.

The expansion of British settlements into the interior of the continent was driven by the search for arable land and resources. Explorers like Matthew Flinders, who circumnavigated Australia and confirmed it as a continent, and later explorers such as Charles Sturt, John McDouall Stuart, and Ludwig Leichhardt, played crucial roles in mapping and opening up the interior for settlement. This expansion often led to conflicts with the Indigenous populations, as European settlers encroached on their traditional lands, disrupting their way of life and leading to violent confrontations.

The impact of British colonization on Indigenous Australians was devastating. The arrival of Europeans brought diseases to which the Indigenous people had no immunity, resulting in significant population declines. Smallpox, influenza, and other diseases decimated communities. Additionally, the introduction of new land use practices, such as agriculture and grazing, disrupted traditional hunting and gathering practices. The displacement from their lands and the loss of access to traditional resources compounded the impact on Indigenous societies. The British colonial authorities often failed to recognize Indigenous land rights and cultural practices, leading to further marginalization and dispossession.

One of the most significant policies affecting Indigenous Australians was the doctrine of terra nullius, which declared that the land was unoccupied prior to British settlement. This legal fiction ignored the presence of Indigenous people and their complex systems of land ownership and management. The doctrine justified the seizure of land without treaties or compensation. Over time, resistance to European encroachment led to conflicts known as the Australian frontier wars. These conflicts, which occurred intermittently from the late 18th century to the early 20th century, involved guerrilla warfare, massacres, and punitive expeditions by both Indigenous groups and European settlers.

The economic development of the Australian colonies was significantly influenced by the discovery of valuable resources. The gold rushes of the 1850s and 1860s, starting with the discovery of gold in New South Wales and Victoria, brought a surge of immigrants from around the world, dramatically increasing the population and transforming the economy. The influx of people seeking fortune led to the rapid growth of towns and cities, the establishment of new businesses, and significant infrastructural developments such as railways and telegraph lines. The gold rushes also stimulated other industries, including agriculture, manufacturing, and services, creating a more diversified economy.

The social fabric of the colonies evolved with the arrival of various immigrant groups. The gold rush era saw the arrival of people from Europe, North America, and China, contributing to a multicultural society. However, this influx also led to social tensions, particularly against Chinese immigrants, who faced discrimination and violence. Anti-Chinese sentiment resulted in restrictive legislation, such as the Chinese Immigration Act of 1855 in Victoria, which aimed to limit Chinese immigration.

Throughout the 19th century, the Australian colonies gradually gained more autonomy from Britain. The establishment of colonial parliaments and the development of self-governing institutions allowed for greater local control over domestic affairs. By the late 19th century, the movement towards federation gained momentum, driven by the desire for a unified defense, economic integration, and national identity. The process culminated in the Federation of Australia on January 1, 1901, when the six separate colonies united to form the Commonwealth of Australia. The new nation retained ties to Britain through the monarchy and membership in the British Empire but enjoyed increased sovereignty and self-determination.

British colonialism also had a lasting cultural impact on Australia. English became the dominant language, and British legal, political, and educational systems were established. The cultural influence extended to literature, art, and social norms, creating a society that, while uniquely Australian, retained strong connections to its British heritage. The legacy of colonialism is reflected in Australia's parliamentary democracy, legal framework, and various cultural traditions.

The effects of British colonialism in Australia continue to be felt today. The legacy of dispossession and marginalization of Indigenous Australians remains a significant issue, with ongoing efforts to address historical injustices and achieve reconciliation. Land rights movements, such as the landmark Mabo decision in 1992, which recognized Indigenous land ownership and overturned the doctrine of terra nullius, represent significant steps towards rectifying past wrongs. Contemporary Australia grapples with the need to acknowledge and reconcile its colonial past while building a more inclusive and equitable society.

In recent decades, there has been a growing recognition of the importance of Indigenous culture and heritage. Efforts to preserve and promote Indigenous languages, traditions, and knowledge systems are gaining momentum. Additionally, initiatives to include Indigenous perspectives in education, media, and public discourse aim to foster greater understanding and respect for the First Nations people of Australia.

The relationship between Australia and Britain has evolved significantly since the colonial era. While historical ties remain strong, characterized by shared institutions, cultural exchanges, and mutual respect, Australia has developed a distinct national identity. The process of decolonization and the pursuit of an independent foreign policy have furthered Australia's role as a sovereign nation on the global stage. The transition from a British colony to an independent country involved not only political and economic changes but also a profound transformation in the national consciousness.

British colonialism in Australia was a period marked by profound changes, challenges, and legacies. The establishment and expansion of European settlements brought about significant economic and social developments while also causing immense suffering and displacement for Indigenous Australians. The journey from a collection of penal colonies to a federated nation highlights the complexities and contradictions of colonialism. Understanding this history is essential for addressing contemporary issues related to reconciliation, national identity, and the enduring impact of colonial legacies on Australian society.

Chapter 13: French Influence in Vietnam

French influence in Vietnam, spanning from the mid-19th century until the mid-20th century, represents a complex period marked by significant political, economic, social, and cultural transformations. The French colonial era in Vietnam began with the initial military invasions in the 1850s and culminated in the eventual establishment of French Indochina, comprising Vietnam, Laos, and Cambodia. This period saw the imposition of French administrative systems, economic exploitation, and cultural imposition, all of which had profound and lasting effects on Vietnamese society.

The origins of French interest in Vietnam can be traced to the 17th century when Catholic missionaries first arrived in the region. These missionaries, primarily Jesuits, played a crucial role in fostering early French ties with Vietnam. Their efforts to convert the Vietnamese population and establish a foothold for Christianity created initial points of contact between the two cultures. However, it was not until the 19th century that France's geopolitical and economic ambitions led to direct intervention.

The initial French incursions into Vietnam were motivated by a combination of religious, economic, and strategic factors. The French sought to protect their missionaries, who faced persecution from Vietnamese authorities wary of foreign influence. At the same time, they aimed to establish trade routes and secure access to resources. The capture of Da Nang in 1858 and subsequent military campaigns led to the Treaty of Saigon in 1862, which ceded control of several southern provinces to France. This marked the beginning of formal French colonial rule in Vietnam.

Over the following decades, French control expanded northward. By 1883, following a series of military engagements and treaties, France had established its dominance over the entire country, consolidating its rule with the formation of French Indochina in 1887. Vietnam was divided into three regions: Cochinchina in the south, Annam in the central region, and Tonkin in the north. Each region had a different administrative structure, but all were subject to French colonial authority.

The French colonial administration implemented significant changes to Vietnam's political and economic structures. Traditional Vietnamese institutions were dismantled or co-opted to serve colonial interests. The administrative system was centralized, with French officials holding key positions and Vietnamese bureaucrats serving in subordinate roles. The legal system was overhauled to reflect French law, often disregarding local customs and traditions.

Economically, the French focused on exploiting Vietnam's natural resources for the benefit of the metropole. They introduced large-scale plantations for rubber, coffee, tea, and rice, employing Vietnamese labor under harsh conditions. Infrastructure development, including the construction of roads, railways, and ports, facilitated the extraction and export of these resources. However, these projects primarily served colonial economic interests rather than the development of the local economy.

The French also sought to transform Vietnamese society through cultural assimilation policies, often referred to as the mission civilisatrice or civilizing mission. This ideology was premised on the belief that French culture and civilization were superior and that it was France's duty to civilize the Vietnamese people. French language and education were promoted, with the establishment of schools and universities modeled on the French system. While these institutions provided some Vietnamese with opportunities for advancement, they also reinforced social hierarchies and created a class of Western-educated elites who were often disconnected from traditional Vietnamese culture.

The introduction of French cultural elements was evident in various aspects of daily life. French architectural styles influenced the design of buildings in cities like Hanoi and Saigon, where colonial-era structures still stand today. French cuisine, fashion, and social customs also left their mark on Vietnamese society. However, this cultural imposition often met with resistance and contributed to a sense of national identity among the Vietnamese.

The impact of French colonial rule on Vietnam was profound and multifaceted, but it also sowed the seeds of resistance and nationalism. The harsh economic exploitation and social inequalities under French rule led to widespread discontent among the Vietnamese population. Early resistance movements, such as the Can Vuong movement in the late 19th century, sought to expel the French and restore traditional Vietnamese authority. Although these early efforts were largely unsuccessful, they laid the groundwork for future nationalist movements.

The early 20th century saw the emergence of more organized and ideologically diverse nationalist movements. Figures like Phan Boi Chau and Phan Chu Trinh advocated for reform and independence through different means. Phan Boi Chau promoted armed struggle and alliances with other anti-colonial forces, while Phan Chu Trinh emphasized education and peaceful reform. Despite their differing approaches, both contributed to the growing sense of Vietnamese nationalism.

The interwar period brought significant changes to the colonial landscape. The global economic depression of the 1930s exacerbated the economic hardships in Vietnam, leading to increased unrest. The rise of communism also had a significant impact, with the formation of the Indochinese Communist Party (ICP) in 1930 under the leadership of Ho Chi Minh. The ICP played a crucial role in organizing labor strikes, peasant uprisings, and other forms of resistance against French rule.

World War II was a turning point in the history of French colonialism in Vietnam. The Japanese occupation of Vietnam from

1940 to 1945 disrupted French control and created a power vacuum. Although the Japanese initially allowed the French to administer Vietnam under their supervision, the situation changed in March 1945 when Japan ousted the French administration and declared Vietnam independent under Emperor Bao Dai. This short-lived independence, however, ended with Japan's defeat in August 1945.

Following Japan's surrender, the Viet Minh, a communist-led nationalist movement led by Ho Chi Minh, seized the opportunity to declare Vietnam's independence on September 2, 1945. The Viet Minh had built a substantial support base during the war through their resistance against Japanese occupation and their efforts to address the needs of the Vietnamese people. However, their declaration of independence was not recognized by the returning French, leading to the outbreak of the First Indochina War in December 1946.

The First Indochina War, which lasted until 1954, was a protracted and brutal conflict between the Viet Minh and French forces. The war ended with the decisive Battle of Dien Bien Phu, where Viet Minh forces defeated the French, leading to the Geneva Accords of 1954. The accords resulted in the temporary division of Vietnam at the 17th parallel, with the Viet Minh controlling the north and a non-communist government in the south, setting the stage for the Vietnam War.

French colonialism in Vietnam had long-lasting effects on the country's political, economic, and social fabric. The colonial era introduced modern infrastructure, education, and administrative systems, but it also entrenched social inequalities and economic exploitation. The experience of colonial rule and the struggle for independence significantly shaped Vietnamese national identity and laid the foundations for future conflicts.

The legacy of French colonialism is still evident in contemporary Vietnam. French architecture, cuisine, and cultural influences can be seen in cities like Hanoi and Ho Chi Minh City. The education system, though reformed, retains some elements of the French model. The colonial period is also a significant part of Vietnamese historical consciousness, informing the country's sense of identity and its relationship with the wider world.

Chapter 14: Russian Expansion into Siberia

Russian expansion into Siberia is a monumental chapter in the history of the Russian Empire, marking a period of vast territorial growth, economic exploitation, and significant cultural interactions. This expansion, spanning from the late 16th century to the early 20th century, saw the transformation of Siberia from a largely uncharted wilderness into a crucial part of the Russian Empire, with profound and lasting effects on both the region and Russia itself.

The initial impetus for Russian expansion into Siberia can be traced back to the late 16th century during the reign of Ivan the Terrible. The conquest began with the overthrow of the Tatar Khanate of Sibir in 1582 by a Cossack expedition led by Yermak Timofeyevich. This victory, which took place near the modern city of Tobolsk, opened the way for further incursions into Siberia. The Russian state saw the region's vast resources as a means to bolster its economy and provide a buffer against potential threats from Central Asia.

Yermak's campaign was largely driven by the Stroganov family, wealthy merchants who financed the expedition in exchange for control over the fur trade in the newly conquered territories. Furs, particularly sable, were in high demand in Europe and represented a lucrative commodity for Russian traders. Following Yermak's initial success, the Russian state supported further expeditions, leading to the gradual annexation of vast tracts of land east of the Ural Mountains.

The expansion was characterized by the establishment of a series of forts and trading posts, which served as centers of Russian control and commerce. These outposts, such as Mangazeya, Tara, and Tobolsk, became the nuclei of Russian presence in Siberia. Tobolsk, founded in 1587, emerged as the administrative center of Siberia and played a crucial role in the colonization efforts. These forts were often situated along major rivers, which provided natural transportation routes into the interior.

The Russian conquest of Siberia involved numerous skirmishes and conflicts with indigenous peoples, such as the Khanty, Mansi, Evenki, and Yakuts, who resisted the encroachments on their lands. Despite the resistance, Russian Cossacks, utilizing their superior weaponry and military tactics, managed to subdue many of these groups. The Russian authorities often imposed yasak, a fur tribute, on the indigenous populations, integrating them into the empire's economic system. This tribute system placed significant economic pressures on the native peoples, altering their traditional ways of life.

The 17th century saw the continuation of Russian expansion, driven by the pursuit of fur, exploration, and the desire to secure territorial control. Russian explorers, such as Semyon Dezhnev, who is believed to have sailed through the Bering Strait in 1648, pushed the boundaries of Russian knowledge and influence. The expeditions of Ivan Moskvitin and Yerofey Khabarov into the Amur River basin further extended Russian claims into the Far East. The establishment of the Ostrog of Yakutsk in 1632 marked a significant milestone, serving as a strategic base for further expansion into the Lena River basin and beyond.

The quest for valuable fur resources continued to drive Russian expansion throughout the 17th century. The exploitation of fur-bearing animals led to the development of a vigorous trade network that extended from the Siberian interior to European markets. This trade was facilitated by the establishment of the Siberian route, or the Great Siberian Road, which connected Moscow to the eastern reaches of the empire. The route facilitated the movement of goods, people, and information, knitting together the vast territories under Russian control.

Russian expansion into Siberia also had profound demographic effects. The settlement of Russian peasants, traders, and adventurers in Siberia brought significant population changes. The Russian government encouraged migration to Siberia through various incentives, including the promise of land and freedom from serfdom. This led to the establishment of numerous villages and towns, contributing to the spread of Russian culture and influence across the region.

The administrative structure of Siberia underwent significant changes as the region was integrated into the Russian Empire. The establishment of the Siberian Department in 1764, headquartered in Irkutsk, marked a formalization of Russian control. This administrative framework facilitated the governance of the vast and diverse territories of Siberia, ensuring the efficient collection of taxes and the maintenance of order.

Economic exploitation of Siberia extended beyond the fur trade. The discovery of valuable mineral resources, such as gold, silver, and iron, spurred further economic development. The Demidov family, prominent Russian industrialists, played a crucial role in developing Siberia's mining industry in the 18th century. The establishment of mining settlements and the construction of infrastructure to support extraction and transportation of minerals underscored Siberia's growing economic significance to the Russian Empire.

The 19th century witnessed the intensification of Russian expansion into Siberia, driven by strategic and geopolitical considerations. The Russian Empire's eastward push culminated in the signing of the Treaty of Nerchinsk with China in 1689, which delineated the borders between the two empires in the Amur region. Further treaties, such as the Treaty of Aigun in 1858 and the Convention of Peking in 1860, expanded Russian control over the Amur and Ussuri regions, solidifying Russian dominance in the Far East.

The construction of the Trans-Siberian Railway, initiated in the late 19th century and completed in the early 20th century, was a transformative project that further integrated Siberia into the Russian Empire. This monumental engineering feat connected European Russia with the Pacific Ocean, facilitating the movement of people, goods, and military forces across the vast expanse of Siberia. The railway spurred economic development, enabling the exploitation of Siberia's vast natural resources, and contributed to the settlement and urbanization of the region.

Cultural and scientific exploration of Siberia also flourished during this period. Russian explorers, scientists, and ethnographers, such as Vitus Bering, Alexander von Middendorff, and Vladimir Arsenyev, conducted extensive surveys and studies of Siberia's geography, flora, fauna, and indigenous cultures. Their work contributed to the broader understanding of Siberia and its integration into the intellectual and scientific currents of the Russian Empire.

The Russian Revolution of 1917 and the subsequent civil war had significant implications for Siberia. The region became a battleground between Bolshevik and anti-Bolshevik forces, leading to widespread turmoil and suffering. The establishment of Soviet power in Siberia brought profound changes, including collectivization, industrialization, and the imposition of communist ideology. The construction of labor camps, or gulags, during the Stalinist era led to the forced migration and suffering of millions, leaving a dark legacy in Siberia's history.

Despite the harsh conditions and political upheavals, Siberia remained a vital part of the Soviet Union's economy and strategic interests. The exploitation of Siberia's vast natural resources, including oil, gas, timber, and minerals, continued to play a crucial role in the Soviet economy. Major industrial cities, such as Novosibirsk, Krasnoyarsk, and Irkutsk, emerged as centers of economic activity and population growth.

The post-Soviet era brought new challenges and opportunities for Siberia. The collapse of the Soviet Union in 1991 led to economic dislocation, political instability, and social upheaval. However, Siberia's rich natural resources continued to attract investment and development. The region's strategic location and economic potential have remained significant for the Russian Federation, contributing to ongoing efforts to integrate Siberia into the global economy.

Chapter 15: Ottoman Control of the Balkans

The Ottoman control of the Balkans represents a significant and complex chapter in the history of Southeastern Europe and the Middle East. Spanning over five centuries, from the late 14th century until the early 20th century, this period witnessed profound political, social, cultural, and economic transformations in the region. The Ottoman Empire's expansion into the Balkans was marked by military conquests, administrative integration, cultural exchanges, and the establishment of a multi-ethnic and multi-religious society. The lasting impact of Ottoman rule on the Balkans continues to be felt and debated to this day.

The origins of Ottoman expansion into the Balkans can be traced back to the early 14th century. The Ottoman state, founded by Osman I in 1299 in northwestern Anatolia, quickly grew into a formidable power under his successors. The strategic location of the Ottoman heartland allowed for both European and Asian conquests. The Balkans, fragmented into numerous principalities and weakened by internal conflicts, presented an appealing target for Ottoman expansion. The Battle of Maritsa in 1371 marked a significant Ottoman victory over a coalition of Balkan rulers, paving the way for further conquests.

One of the most pivotal moments in the Ottoman conquest of the Balkans was the Battle of Kosovo in 1389. Despite the mythologized nature of this battle in Balkan national histories, it resulted in a strategic Ottoman victory and the subsequent vassalage of Serbian territories. The fall of the Bulgarian Empire in 1393 and the conquest of the Serbian Despotate in 1459 further solidified Ottoman control. The capture of Constantinople in 1453 by Mehmed the Conqueror not only marked the end of the Byzantine Empire but also provided the Ottomans with a crucial strategic and symbolic capital, enabling further expansion into Europe.

The administrative organization of the Balkans under Ottoman rule was characterized by the incorporation of the region into the wider imperial structure through a system of provincial governance known as the vilayet system. The Balkans were divided into several provinces, each governed by a beylerbey or pasha, who was responsible for maintaining order, collecting taxes, and overseeing local administration. The timar system, a form of land tenure, was introduced, whereby military officers were granted land in exchange for their service. This system helped integrate local elites into the Ottoman military and administrative apparatus, ensuring their loyalty to the empire.

Religious and cultural policies played a crucial role in the Ottoman administration of the Balkans. The Ottomans employed a pragmatic approach to religion, allowing a considerable degree of religious autonomy to Christian and Jewish communities through the millet system. Each religious community, or millet, was granted the right to govern its own affairs, maintain its religious institutions, and apply its own legal codes in matters of personal status. This system facilitated the coexistence of diverse religious groups within the empire, although it also reinforced communal boundaries.

The spread of Islam in the Balkans was a gradual and multifaceted process. While the Ottomans encouraged conversion through various means, such as tax incentives and social mobility opportunities, they generally did not enforce mass conversions. The establishment of Islamic institutions, such as mosques, madrasas, and Sufi tekkes, played a significant role in the cultural and religious life of the region. Prominent Ottoman architectural achievements, such as the Selimiye Mosque in Edirne and the Gazi Husrev-beg Mosque in Sarajevo, became enduring symbols of Ottoman influence.

Economic policies under Ottoman rule were designed to integrate the Balkans into the broader imperial economy. The region's rich agricultural land and strategic location facilitated the production and trade of various goods, including grains, livestock, and textiles. The establishment of caravanserais and markets promoted regional and long-distance trade, connecting the Balkans with other parts of the Ottoman Empire and beyond. Major cities like Thessaloniki, Sarajevo, and Belgrade emerged as important commercial and cultural centers.

Social and demographic changes were also significant during Ottoman rule. The Ottoman system of governance encouraged the settlement of diverse groups, including Turks, Albanians, Greeks, Slavs, Vlachs, and Jews, leading to a vibrant mosaic of cultures and identities. The practice of devshirme, the periodic levy of Christian boys who were converted to Islam and trained for military or administrative service, played a crucial role in the Ottoman military and bureaucratic structure. These individuals, known as Janissaries, often rose to prominent positions within the empire, further integrating the Balkans into the Ottoman system.

Despite the relative stability and prosperity brought by Ottoman rule, the Balkans also experienced periods of conflict and resistance. The rise of nationalist movements in the 19th century, fueled by Enlightenment ideas and inspired by the success of the Greek War of Independence (1821-1829), posed significant challenges to Ottoman authority. The decline of the Ottoman Empire, exacerbated by military defeats, internal corruption, and economic difficulties, provided fertile ground for the emergence of nationalist aspirations among Balkan peoples.

The late 19th and early 20th centuries were marked by a series of nationalist uprisings and wars that ultimately led to the disintegration of Ottoman control in the Balkans. The Russo-Turkish War (1877-1878) resulted in significant territorial losses for the Ottomans and the establishment of independent or autonomous states, including

Romania, Serbia, Montenegro, and Bulgaria. The Balkan Wars of 1912-1913 further accelerated the collapse of Ottoman rule, as Balkan states united to drive the Ottomans out of their remaining European territories.

The legacy of Ottoman rule in the Balkans is complex and multifaceted. On one hand, the Ottomans contributed to the region's cultural and architectural heritage, economic development, and social diversity. The coexistence of various religious and ethnic communities under the millet system left a lasting impact on the region's identity. On the other hand, the imposition of Ottoman authority and the practice of devshirme are often viewed negatively in nationalist narratives, which emphasize the struggle for independence and the preservation of local traditions.

The post-Ottoman period in the Balkans was characterized by significant upheaval and transformation. The formation of new nation-states, the redrawing of borders, and the integration of the region into the global political and economic system brought new challenges and opportunities. The legacy of Ottoman rule continued to shape the political, social, and cultural dynamics of the Balkans, as communities grappled with the memory of imperial rule and the construction of new national identities.

Chapter 16: British Domination of Egypt

British domination of Egypt, spanning from 1882 until the mid-20th century, was a period marked by significant political, economic, and social transformations. This era began with the British occupation of Egypt, a strategic move driven by a combination of imperial ambition, economic interests, and geopolitical considerations, particularly concerning the Suez Canal, a critical maritime route connecting the Mediterranean Sea with the Red Sea and beyond to the Indian Ocean.

The roots of British interest in Egypt can be traced back to the early 19th century, when the country was undergoing modernization under the rule of Muhammad Ali Pasha. Recognizing Egypt's strategic importance, the British sought to secure their interests in the region, particularly as European powers were competing for influence in the Middle East and North Africa. The construction of the Suez Canal, completed in 1869, further heightened British interest, as the canal significantly shortened the sea route between Europe and Asia, becoming vital for British trade, particularly with India.

Economic issues in Egypt in the late 19th century played a crucial role in setting the stage for British intervention. Excessive borrowing to finance ambitious modernization projects led to severe debt problems. By the 1870s, Egypt was unable to meet its financial obligations, resulting in increased European control over its economy. A commission was established to oversee Egypt's finances, with Britain and France playing leading roles. This period of financial oversight paved the way for deeper political intervention.

The immediate catalyst for British occupation was the nationalist uprising led by Colonel Ahmed Urabi in 1881-1882. Urabi's revolt, driven by discontent among the military and civilian population against foreign interference and the ruling Khedive Tewfik Pasha's policies, threatened European interests in Egypt. The British, concerned about the security of the Suez Canal and their broader imperial interests, decided to intervene militarily. In 1882, British forces defeated Urabi's forces at the Battle of Tel el-Kebir and occupied Cairo, effectively placing Egypt under British control.

The British administration in Egypt, though nominally under the suzerainty of the Ottoman Empire, was effectively autonomous. The British installed a system of indirect rule, maintaining the facade of Egyptian sovereignty while exerting significant control over the country's governance. The Khedive remained the official ruler, but real power was held by the British Consul-General, the most notable of whom was Lord Cromer (Evelyn Baring), who served from 1883 to 1907.

Under British rule, Egypt underwent significant economic changes. The British focused on developing Egypt's agricultural sector, particularly cotton production, which was crucial for British textile mills. Investments in irrigation infrastructure, such as the construction of the Aswan Dam in 1902, aimed to increase agricultural output. While these projects boosted cotton production, they also reinforced Egypt's dependency on a single cash crop, making its economy vulnerable to fluctuations in global cotton prices.

The British also implemented reforms in administration, education, and public health. They sought to modernize the bureaucratic apparatus, introducing measures to improve efficiency and reduce corruption. However, these reforms often prioritized British interests and the stability of colonial rule over the welfare of the Egyptian population. Educational reforms aimed at creating a cadre of local administrators loyal to the British, while public health initiatives were motivated by the need to maintain a healthy workforce for the agricultural and infrastructure projects.

Socially, British rule had profound impacts on Egyptian society. The British introduced Western legal and administrative practices, which often clashed with traditional Islamic and local customs. The British presence also exacerbated social stratification, with a small elite benefiting from British policies while the majority of the population, particularly peasants, faced exploitation and hardship. Land concentration in the hands of a few large landowners, often with British connections, marginalized small farmers and contributed to rural poverty.

Nationalism and resistance to British rule grew over the decades. The early 20th century saw the rise of nationalist movements, driven by a desire for independence and self-determination. The Dinshaway Incident in 1906, where British officers clashed with villagers leading to harsh reprisals, galvanized nationalist sentiments and highlighted the oppressive nature of British rule. Political organizations such as the Wafd Party, founded in 1919, played a leading role in the struggle for independence, advocating for constitutional reforms and greater political representation.

World War I marked a turning point in the British-Egyptian relationship. During the war, Egypt was declared a British protectorate, further tightening British control. The war strained Egypt's economy and led to increased demands for resources and manpower, exacerbating social tensions. The post-war period saw a surge in nationalist activity, culminating in the 1919 Revolution. Widespread protests and strikes demanded an end to British rule and the establishment of an independent constitutional government. The revolution forced the British to reconsider their policies.

In response to the 1919 Revolution, the British issued the Unilateral Declaration of Egyptian Independence in 1922, ending the protectorate status and declaring Egypt an independent kingdom. However, British influence remained significant, particularly in defense, foreign policy, and the Suez Canal. The Anglo-Egyptian Treaty of 1936 granted Egypt greater autonomy but allowed British troops to remain in the country, ensuring continued British strategic interests were protected.

The interwar period saw continued nationalist agitation and political instability. The Wafd Party, led by figures like Saad Zaghloul, dominated Egyptian politics, advocating for full independence and democratic reforms. However, tensions between the monarchy, the Wafd, and the British complicated efforts to achieve meaningful change. The outbreak of World War II further highlighted Egypt's strategic importance, as the country became a key base for Allied operations in the Middle East and North Africa.

The post-war period was marked by intensified nationalist demands and anti-British sentiment. The rise of the Free Officers Movement, a group of nationalist military officers, culminated in the 1952 coup d'état led by General Muhammad Naguib and Gamal Abdel Nasser. The coup overthrew King Farouk and established a republic, ending the monarchy and paving the way for significant social, economic, and political reforms.

One of the most significant events during this period was the Suez Crisis of 1956. In response to Nasser's nationalization of the Suez Canal, Britain, France, and Israel launched a military intervention to regain control. The crisis ended with a political defeat for the intervening powers, as international pressure, particularly from the United States and the Soviet Union, forced them to withdraw. The Suez Crisis marked the end of British imperial influence in Egypt and underscored the shift in global power dynamics during the Cold War era.

The legacy of British domination in Egypt is multifaceted. British rule left a lasting impact on Egypt's political, economic, and social structures. The emphasis on cotton production and infrastructure development shaped the country's economic trajectory, while the introduction of Western legal and administrative practices influenced its governance. The nationalist struggle against British rule played a crucial role in shaping modern Egyptian identity and the quest for independence and self-determination.

However, British domination also had negative consequences. The focus on cotton production and the concentration of land ownership exacerbated economic inequalities and rural poverty. The imposition of foreign rule and the suppression of nationalist movements contributed to social and political tensions. The legacy of colonialism continues to influence contemporary debates about Egypt's development, governance, and national identity.

Chapter 17: Spanish Rule in the Philippines

The Spanish rule in the Philippines, spanning over three centuries from 1565 to 1898, was a period marked by profound transformations in the archipelago's political, social, cultural, and economic landscapes. This era began with the arrival of Spanish explorers and culminated in the Philippine Revolution and the subsequent cession of the Philippines to the United States. The legacy of Spanish colonial rule in the Philippines is complex, reflecting a blend of exploitation and development, resistance and assimilation.

The initial contact between Spain and the Philippines occurred in 1521 when Ferdinand Magellan, a Portuguese explorer sailing under the Spanish flag, arrived in the archipelago. Magellan's expedition was part of Spain's broader efforts to explore and claim new territories in the wake of Columbus's discovery of the Americas. Although Magellan himself was killed in the Battle of Mactan, his voyage marked the beginning of Spain's interest in the region. It wasn't until 1565, however, that Spain established a permanent settlement in the Philippines under the leadership of Miguel López de Legazpi, who founded the city of Cebu.

The primary motivations for Spanish colonization of the Philippines were multifaceted. Spain sought to expand its empire, spread Christianity, and establish a strategic base for trade and military operations in Asia. The Philippines' location made it an ideal staging ground for Spanish interests in the Pacific, particularly in relation to the lucrative spice trade and the galleon trade between Manila and Acapulco, which became a cornerstone of Spanish colonial economy.

Spanish colonization profoundly altered the political structure of the Philippines. The Spanish implemented a centralized colonial government, replacing the fragmented and independent barangays (village communities) ruled by local chieftains known as datus. The archipelago was organized into provinces headed by Spanish governors, and local governance was entrusted to encomenderos, who were granted control over land and the indigenous population in exchange for their services to the crown. This system, known as the encomienda, facilitated the extraction of tribute and labor from the native Filipinos, known as indios.

The imposition of Spanish rule was met with varying degrees of resistance from the indigenous population. While some local leaders allied with the Spanish for political and economic advantage, others fiercely resisted foreign domination. Notable revolts during the early colonial period included the Lakandula and Soliman Revolt in Manila (1574) and the Dagami Revolt in Cebu (1567). These uprisings, though ultimately unsuccessful, underscored the widespread discontent with Spanish rule and the imposition of foreign authority.

A significant aspect of Spanish colonization was the widespread conversion of the indigenous population to Christianity. Missionaries from various religious orders, including the Augustinians, Franciscans, Jesuits, and Dominicans, played a crucial role in the evangelization of the archipelago. Churches, convents, and schools were established across the islands, becoming centers of religious and social life. The introduction of Christianity profoundly impacted Filipino culture, leading to the syncretism of indigenous beliefs and Catholic practices. The establishment of Catholicism also had long-lasting effects on Filipino identity and societal norms.

The economic policies of the Spanish colonial administration were primarily extractive, designed to benefit the Spanish crown and colonial elite. The galleon trade, which operated from 1565 to 1815, linked Manila and Acapulco, facilitating the exchange of Asian goods, such as silk and spices, for silver from the Americas. This trade brought wealth to Manila, transforming it into a cosmopolitan hub, but it also entrenched economic dependency and limited the development of local industries. The encomienda system and later the hacienda system concentrated land ownership in the hands of a few, leading to widespread peasant exploitation and agrarian unrest.

Social stratification under Spanish rule was pronounced. At the top of the social hierarchy were the peninsulares, Spaniards born in Spain, followed by the insulares or criollos, Spaniards born in the Philippines. Below them were the mestizos, individuals of mixed Spanish and indigenous descent, who often held significant economic and social influence. The majority of the population comprised the indios, who faced heavy taxation, forced labor, and limited social mobility. This rigid class structure perpetuated social inequalities and fueled resentment among the native population.

The 19th century brought significant changes to the Philippines under Spanish rule. The opening of Manila to international trade in 1834 and the development of cash-crop agriculture, such as sugar, tobacco, and abaca, integrated the Philippine economy more closely with global markets. This period also saw the rise of a Filipino middle class, composed of educated and wealthy mestizos and indios, who began to challenge Spanish colonial authority. The spread of liberal ideas from Europe, the rise of the ilustrados (enlightened ones), and increasing dissatisfaction with colonial policies contributed to the growing nationalist sentiment.

The seeds of revolution were sown in the late 19th century with the emergence of reformist and revolutionary movements. The Propaganda Movement, led by Filipino intellectuals such as José Rizal, Marcelo H. del Pilar, and Graciano López Jaena, advocated for political reforms, greater representation, and social equality. They used newspapers, books, and pamphlets to raise awareness and mobilize support among Filipinos. Despite their efforts, the Spanish colonial government largely ignored their demands, leading to increased radicalization.

The outbreak of the Philippine Revolution in 1896 marked a turning point in the struggle for independence. Led by the secret society Katipunan, founded by Andrés Bonifacio, the revolution sought to overthrow Spanish rule through armed resistance. The execution of José Rizal, a leading figure of the Propaganda Movement, by Spanish authorities in 1896 further galvanized the revolutionary cause. Emilio Aguinaldo emerged as a key leader, and under his command, Filipino forces scored significant victories against the Spanish.

The Spanish-American War in 1898 had a profound impact on the Philippines. The defeat of Spain by the United States led to the signing of the Treaty of Paris, under which Spain ceded the Philippines to the United States for $20 million. Filipino revolutionaries, who had declared independence and established the First Philippine Republic under Aguinaldo, found themselves facing a new colonial power. The subsequent Philippine-American War from 1899 to 1902 resulted in the establishment of American colonial rule, marking the end of Spanish sovereignty in the archipelago.

The legacy of Spanish rule in the Philippines is multifaceted and enduring. On one hand, Spanish colonization introduced new technologies, crops, and cultural practices that contributed to the development of Philippine society. The spread of Christianity and the establishment of educational institutions had lasting impacts on Filipino culture and identity. Spanish influence is evident in the Filipino language, with many Spanish loanwords integrated into Tagalog and other local languages.

However, the negative aspects of Spanish rule cannot be overlooked. The exploitative economic policies, social stratification, and harsh treatment of the indigenous population left deep scars. The concentration of land ownership and the suppression of local industries stunted economic development and entrenched poverty. The struggle for independence and the resistance against colonial oppression became defining aspects of Filipino nationalism and identity.

Chapter 18: Dutch Colonization of South Africa

Dutch colonization of South Africa, which began in the mid-17th century, marks a significant chapter in the history of colonialism. This era, starting with the establishment of the Dutch East India Company (VOC) settlement at the Cape of Good Hope in 1652, profoundly influenced the region's socio-economic, cultural, and political landscape. The VOC, a powerful trading entity, initially intended the Cape to serve as a refreshment station for its ships en route to the East Indies. However, this strategic outpost quickly transformed into a permanent settlement due to its advantageous location and the fertile land that offered promising agricultural prospects.

The establishment of the Dutch settlement was spearheaded by Jan van Riebeeck, who arrived with a small group of VOC employees. Their primary mission was to secure a supply station to replenish the VOC's ships with fresh water, meat, vegetables, and fruit, thereby ensuring healthier and more efficient sea voyages. Over time, this foothold expanded as more settlers, including freed VOC employees and their families, arrived. These settlers, known as the Free Burghers, were granted land to cultivate and develop farms, marking the beginning of an agricultural society that would grow in size and influence.

One of the most significant impacts of Dutch colonization was on the indigenous Khoikhoi and San populations. The arrival of the Dutch settlers led to conflicts over land and resources, as the expanding European settlements encroached on the territories traditionally inhabited and used by the indigenous peoples. The Dutch introduced new agricultural practices, livestock, and crops, fundamentally altering the landscape and economy. This led to a disruption of the Khoikhoi's pastoralist lifestyle and resulted in numerous conflicts, often culminating in violent confrontations and forced dispossession of land.

Slavery became an integral part of the Cape Colony's labor system, with the Dutch importing slaves from other parts of Africa, Madagascar, and the East Indies. These slaves played a crucial role in the colony's economy, working on farms, in households, and in various trades. The introduction of slavery not only provided the necessary labor force for the expanding agricultural and economic activities but also had lasting social and cultural implications. The diverse origins of the slaves contributed to the cultural melting pot that characterized the colony, influencing language, cuisine, and social practices.

Dutch colonization also left a lasting legacy on the legal and administrative systems in South Africa. The Dutch legal system, based on Roman-Dutch law, was introduced and became the foundation of the colony's legal framework. This legal tradition has endured and continues to influence South African law to this day. The administrative practices established by the Dutch, including land distribution and governance structures, laid the groundwork for future colonial administrations, including that of the British who took control of the Cape Colony in the early 19th century.

The religious landscape of South Africa was also shaped by Dutch colonization. The Dutch Reformed Church was established as the official church of the colony, and its doctrines and practices influenced the spiritual and moral life of the settlers. The church played a central role in community life, education, and social services, reinforcing Dutch cultural and religious norms. Missionary activities, although limited during the early period of colonization, began to take root, aiming to convert and 'civilize' the indigenous populations and slaves according to European Christian values.

The Dutch colonization period also saw the introduction of Dutch language and culture, which have had a lasting impact on South African society. Afrikaans, a language that developed from Dutch, emerged as a distinct linguistic identity over the centuries, influenced by the interactions between Dutch settlers, indigenous peoples, and slaves. Afrikaans became a significant cultural and political force in South Africa, particularly in the 20th century, as it was embraced by Afrikaner nationalists seeking to assert their identity and heritage.

Economic activities during the Dutch colonial period were diverse, ranging from agriculture to trade and commerce. The Cape's strategic location made it a crucial point for maritime trade routes, facilitating the exchange of goods between Europe, Asia, and other parts of Africa. The Dutch introduced viticulture, and the wine industry became one of the key economic sectors, with vineyards established in areas such as Stellenbosch and Constantia. The export of wine and other agricultural products contributed to the colony's economic growth and integration into the global economy.

The interactions between the Dutch settlers and the indigenous populations, as well as the imported slaves, led to a complex social hierarchy and a multicultural society. Despite the conflicts and tensions, there were instances of intermarriage and cultural exchange, which further shaped the colony's social fabric. However, the colonial administration and settler society were characterized by racial and social stratification, with Europeans occupying the top tiers of the social hierarchy, followed by free blacks, mixed-race individuals, and slaves. This stratified society laid the foundations for the racial divisions and inequalities that would later be entrenched under apartheid.

The Dutch also engaged in expeditions and explorations into the interior of South Africa, driven by the search for new trade routes, resources, and opportunities for expansion. These explorations led to the mapping and understanding of the region's geography, resources, and potential for further colonization. The encounters with various indigenous groups during these expeditions often resulted in the establishment of trade relations, alliances, and sometimes conflicts, further shaping the dynamics of colonial expansion.

Dutch colonization of South Africa set the stage for subsequent European colonial endeavors in the region. The legacy of Dutch rule, particularly in terms of land ownership, legal frameworks, and social structures, continued to influence South African society long after the Dutch relinquished control. The British takeover of the Cape Colony in 1806 marked the end of Dutch political dominance, but the cultural and institutional imprints of Dutch colonization remained deeply embedded.

The enduring impact of Dutch colonization can be seen in the cultural, linguistic, and social heritage of modern South Africa. Afrikaans, as a language and cultural identity, remains an integral part of South African society. The architectural styles, place names, and agricultural practices introduced by the Dutch continue to shape the country's landscape and heritage. The complexities of Dutch colonial history, including the legacy of slavery, land dispossession, and cultural exchange, continue to be subjects of study, reflection, and debate, highlighting the profound and multifaceted influence of this period on South Africa's development.

Chapter 19: French Presence in Morocco

The French presence in Morocco, spanning from the early 20th century to the mid-20th century, represents a significant chapter in the history of North African colonialism. The French established their control over Morocco through a combination of diplomatic maneuvering, military intervention, and strategic alliances, fundamentally altering the political, economic, and social landscape of the country. The story begins in the late 19th century when European powers, particularly France and Spain, eyed Morocco as a valuable strategic asset due to its geographic location and potential economic resources.

The Moroccan Sultanate, under the rule of Sultan Abdelaziz, faced internal strife and mounting pressure from European powers seeking to extend their influence. France's interest in Morocco was driven by a desire to secure its interests in North Africa, protect its Algerian colony, and counter the influence of other European powers, notably Germany. The strategic importance of Morocco's ports and its proximity to vital maritime routes made it an attractive target for French expansion. In 1904, France and Spain reached a secret agreement, known as the Entente Cordiale, which delineated their respective spheres of influence in Morocco. This agreement laid the groundwork for future French intervention.

The situation in Morocco reached a critical point with the Algeciras Conference of 1906, convened to address the Moroccan crisis and the competing interests of European powers. The conference, attended by representatives from major European nations, the United States, and Morocco, aimed to establish a framework for Moroccan independence while acknowledging French and Spanish interests. The resulting Algeciras Act recognized the sovereignty of the Moroccan Sultan but granted France and Spain policing powers and control over key financial and economic institutions. This act marked the beginning of formal European involvement in Moroccan affairs.

Despite the Algeciras Act, tensions persisted, leading to increased French intervention. In 1911, a rebellion against the Sultan in Fez prompted the French to send troops to protect their citizens and interests, effectively establishing a military presence in the country. The Agadir Crisis of the same year further escalated tensions when Germany dispatched a gunboat to Agadir, challenging French influence. The crisis was resolved through negotiations, with Germany recognizing French predominance in Morocco in exchange for territorial concessions in other parts of Africa. This resolution paved the way for the Treaty of Fez in 1912, which formally established the French Protectorate over Morocco. The treaty effectively divided Morocco into French and Spanish zones of influence, with the Sultan retaining nominal authority while real power rested with the French and Spanish administrators.

Under the protectorate system, France implemented significant administrative, economic, and social reforms aimed at modernizing Morocco and integrating it into the French colonial empire. The French administration, led by Resident-General Hubert Lyautey, sought to maintain traditional Moroccan institutions while introducing European-style governance and infrastructure. Lyautey's approach, known as the "policy of association," emphasized cooperation with the Moroccan elite and respect for local customs and traditions. This strategy was intended to minimize resistance and facilitate the gradual transformation of Moroccan society.

One of the key aspects of French rule was the development of infrastructure and urban planning. The French invested heavily in the construction of roads, railways, ports, and public buildings, transforming the Moroccan landscape. The creation of modern cities, such as Casablanca and Rabat, exemplified French urban planning principles and served as centers of administration, commerce, and industry. The development of these urban areas facilitated economic growth and the integration of Morocco into the global economy.

Economic policies under French rule focused on exploiting Morocco's natural resources and agricultural potential. The French introduced new agricultural techniques, encouraged the cultivation of cash crops such as citrus fruits and olives, and established agricultural research stations. These initiatives aimed to increase productivity and generate revenue for the colonial administration. Additionally, French companies invested in mining, particularly in the extraction of phosphates, which became a significant export commodity. The development of the mining sector brought economic benefits but also led to the displacement of local communities and environmental degradation.

French rule also had profound social and cultural impacts on Moroccan society. The introduction of the French education system aimed to create a bilingual elite capable of serving in the colonial administration and bridging the gap between French and Moroccan cultures. French became the language of administration, education, and commerce, creating a cultural divide between those who had access to French education and the broader population. This policy of cultural assimilation, known as the "mission civilisatrice," sought to inculcate French values and norms, but it also sparked resistance and a desire to preserve Moroccan identity and traditions.

The French presence in Morocco was not without resistance and opposition. Various nationalist movements emerged, advocating for independence and the preservation of Moroccan sovereignty. The nationalist movement, led by figures such as Allal al-Fassi and the Istiqlal Party, gained momentum in the 1930s and 1940s, demanding political reforms, the end of the protectorate, and full independence. The movement drew support from various segments of society, including intellectuals, students, and religious leaders, who saw French rule as an affront to Moroccan identity and Islamic values.

The period following World War II saw increased nationalist agitation and demands for independence. The global context of decolonization, coupled with domestic pressure, forced the French to reconsider their position in Morocco. In 1953, the French administration exiled Sultan Mohammed V, who was seen as a symbol of Moroccan resistance, and installed a more pliable ruler. This move backfired, galvanizing nationalist sentiments and leading to widespread protests and unrest. The return of Sultan Mohammed V in 1955, following negotiations with the French, marked a turning point in the struggle for independence.

Morocco finally achieved independence on March 2, 1956, following negotiations between the French government and Moroccan nationalists. The end of the protectorate marked the beginning of a new era for Morocco, as the country embarked on the challenging path of building a modern, independent state. The legacy of French colonial rule, however, continued to influence Morocco's political, economic, and social development. The infrastructure, institutions, and legal frameworks established during the colonial period remained integral to the functioning of the modern state.

The French presence in Morocco left a complex and multifaceted legacy. While French rule brought about significant modernization and economic development, it also led to social stratification, cultural assimilation, and resistance. The impact of the French language and education system persists in contemporary Morocco, influencing the country's intellectual and cultural landscape. The nationalist struggle for independence, shaped by the experience of colonialism, continues to inspire contemporary political movements and the ongoing quest for social justice and national identity.

In the post-independence period, Morocco has sought to navigate its colonial legacy while forging a path toward modernization and development. The relationship between France and Morocco has evolved into one of cooperation and partnership, with France remaining a key economic and political ally. The historical ties between the two countries, shaped by the colonial experience, continue to influence bilateral relations and Morocco's position within the broader international community. The French presence in Morocco, with its enduring impact on the country's development, remains a subject of study and reflection, highlighting the complexities and contradictions of colonial history.

Chapter 20: British Control of Kenya

The British control of Kenya, which began in the late 19th century and lasted until the mid-20th century, is a profound chapter in the history of colonialism in Africa. The British involvement in Kenya was initially driven by strategic interests and the desire to protect trade routes to India and other parts of the British Empire. This period of colonial rule brought about significant changes in Kenya's political, economic, social, and cultural landscape, leaving a legacy that continues to influence the country today.

The origins of British control in Kenya can be traced back to the Berlin Conference of 1884-1885, where European powers convened to divide Africa into spheres of influence without considering existing African societies and political boundaries. During this conference, the region that would become Kenya was allocated to the British, and by the late 1880s, the British East Africa Company (BEAC) was established to administer the territory. The BEAC, a chartered company, sought to exploit the region's resources and establish trade routes, but it faced significant challenges, including resistance from local communities and the harsh climate.

In 1895, the British government assumed direct control of the territory, declaring it the East Africa Protectorate. This marked the beginning of formal colonial rule. One of the first major undertakings by the British was the construction of the Uganda Railway, which aimed to connect the port city of Mombasa to Lake Victoria and facilitate the movement of goods and people. The railway project, completed in 1901, was a monumental engineering feat, but it also brought about profound changes to the region. Thousands of laborers, including many from India, were brought in to work on the railway, contributing to the diverse demographic makeup of Kenya.

The construction of the railway had significant economic and social impacts. It opened up the interior of Kenya to European settlers and commercial agriculture, particularly the cultivation of cash crops such as coffee and tea. The fertile highlands of central Kenya, known as the White Highlands, were designated for European settlement, leading to the displacement of indigenous communities and the appropriation of their land. This land alienation had long-lasting repercussions, creating economic disparities and contributing to social tensions.

The colonial administration implemented various policies to support the settler economy and maintain control over the indigenous population. One such policy was the imposition of hut taxes and other forms of taxation, which forced Africans to engage in the cash economy and seek wage labor on European farms and plantations. Additionally, the British introduced a system of indirect rule, whereby traditional leaders were co-opted into the colonial administration and used to enforce colonial policies. This system often undermined traditional authority and created new power dynamics within African communities.

Education and missionary activities were also significant aspects of British rule in Kenya. Missionaries played a crucial role in the spread of Christianity and Western education. Mission schools, established by various Christian denominations, provided basic education and vocational training but also sought to inculcate European values and norms. The spread of Christianity and Western education contributed to the erosion of traditional beliefs and practices, leading to cultural transformations within Kenyan society.

Resistance to British rule emerged early on and took various forms, ranging from armed rebellions to passive resistance and political organization. One of the most notable early uprisings was the Nandi Resistance (1895-1905), led by the Nandi people under the leadership of Koitalel Arap Samoei. The Nandi fiercely resisted the construction of the Uganda Railway through their territory and the encroachment of European settlers. The British responded with military force, and the resistance was eventually suppressed, leading to the further entrenchment of colonial rule.

Throughout the early 20th century, various African leaders and organizations began to advocate for greater political rights and representation. The formation of associations such as the East African Association (EAA) in 1921, led by Harry Thuku, marked the beginning of organized political activism. Thuku and his followers demanded an end to land alienation, the reduction of taxes, and better working conditions for African laborers. The colonial government responded with repression, culminating in the arrest of Thuku and a violent crackdown on his supporters during the 1922 Nairobi protests.

The interwar period saw the growth of African political consciousness and the formation of more sophisticated political organizations. The Kikuyu Central Association (KCA), founded in 1924, emerged as a prominent voice for African grievances, particularly focusing on land issues and the preservation of Kikuyu culture. Leaders such as Jomo Kenyatta, who would later become Kenya's first president, played a key role in articulating African demands for self-determination and political representation.

The post-World War II period marked a significant turning point in the struggle for independence. The war had exposed the contradictions of colonial rule, as Africans who had fought alongside Europeans for freedom and democracy returned to a colonial system that denied them those very rights. The economic hardships and social changes brought about by the war further fueled discontent. The formation of the Kenya African Union (KAU) in 1944, with Jomo Kenyatta as its leader, marked a new phase in the nationalist movement, as it called for immediate independence and the end of colonial rule.

The struggle for independence reached its peak with the outbreak of the Mau Mau Uprising (1952-1960). The Mau Mau movement, primarily composed of Kikuyu fighters, waged a guerrilla war against the colonial government and European settlers. The movement was driven by deep-seated grievances over land dispossession, economic exploitation, and political marginalization. The British response to the uprising was brutal, involving mass arrests, detentions, and the establishment of concentration camps where suspected Mau Mau supporters were subjected to harsh conditions and torture.

The Mau Mau Uprising had a profound impact on the course of Kenyan history. It galvanized nationalist sentiments and drew international attention to the injustices of colonial rule. The British government, facing mounting pressure both domestically and internationally, began to reconsider its position in Kenya. The Lyttelton Constitution of 1954 and subsequent constitutional reforms aimed to address African grievances by increasing African representation in the Legislative Council. However, these reforms were seen as too little, too late, and the demand for full independence continued to grow.

The negotiations for independence intensified in the late 1950s and early 1960s, culminating in the Lancaster House Conferences, where African leaders and representatives of the colonial government hammered out the details of the transition to self-rule. On December 12, 1963, Kenya officially gained independence, with Jomo Kenyatta becoming the country's first prime minister, and later its first president. The end of British colonial rule marked the beginning of a new era for Kenya, as the country embarked on the challenging task of nation-building and addressing the legacies of colonialism.

The British control of Kenya left a lasting legacy on the country's political, economic, and social landscape. The colonial period was marked by the creation of a dual economy, with a modern, export-oriented sector dominated by European settlers and a subsistence sector populated by African farmers. This economic structure created disparities that persisted long after independence. The legacy of land alienation and the concentration of land in the hands of a few remained a contentious issue, fueling land conflicts and social tensions.

The introduction of Western education and Christianity had profound cultural impacts, leading to the erosion of traditional beliefs and practices while also creating a Western-educated elite that would play a crucial role in post-independence Kenya. The political institutions and administrative structures established during colonial rule provided the framework for the independent state, but they also reflected the authoritarian and hierarchical nature of colonial governance, influencing post-independence political developments.

The struggle for independence, epitomized by the Mau Mau Uprising, became a symbol of Kenyan resistance and resilience. The narratives of resistance and liberation have continued to shape Kenyan national identity and political discourse. The experiences of colonial rule and the fight for freedom have been commemorated and remembered through literature, music, and other forms of cultural expression, contributing to a collective memory of the colonial past.

In the post-independence period, Kenya has faced numerous challenges in addressing the legacies of colonialism while striving for development and modernization. The issues of land reform, economic inequality, and political representation remain central to the country's political agenda. The relationship between Kenya and the former colonial power, Britain, has evolved into one of partnership and cooperation, with continued economic, cultural, and diplomatic ties.

The British control of Kenya is a complex and multifaceted chapter in the country's history, marked by exploitation, resistance, and eventual liberation. The impacts of this period continue to resonate in contemporary Kenya, shaping its socio-economic and political landscape. The study of this era provides valuable insights into the dynamics of colonialism and the enduring legacies of colonial rule in Africa. The experiences of Kenya under British rule highlight the resilience and agency of the Kenyan people in their quest for self-determination and justice.

Chapter 21: Portuguese Colonization of Angola

The Portuguese colonization of Angola, spanning several centuries, is a profound and complex chapter in the history of African colonialism. The Portuguese first arrived in Angola in the late 15th century, initiating a period of intense exploration, trade, and ultimately colonization that would shape the region's political, economic, and social landscapes. The legacy of Portuguese rule has left an indelible mark on Angola, influencing its contemporary identity, challenges, and development trajectory.

The Portuguese exploration of Africa began in earnest in the mid-15th century, driven by a desire to find new trade routes, access gold and other valuable resources, and spread Christianity. In 1482, the Portuguese navigator Diogo Cão reached the mouth of the Congo River, establishing initial contact with the powerful Kingdom of Kongo. This contact marked the beginning of Portuguese involvement in the region that would become Angola. The Kingdom of Kongo, located in present-day northern Angola and parts of the Democratic Republic of the Congo, was a sophisticated and well-organized state with which the Portuguese established diplomatic and trade relations.

The early Portuguese presence in Angola was primarily focused on trade, particularly in slaves. The transatlantic slave trade, which began in the 16th century, had a devastating impact on Angola and its people. Portuguese traders, in collaboration with African intermediaries, captured and transported millions of Angolans to the Americas, where they were sold into slavery. The demand for slaves in the Americas, driven by the plantation economies of Brazil, the Caribbean, and North America, fueled the expansion of the slave trade in Angola. This trade not only decimated the local population but also disrupted traditional societies and economies.

In the early stages of Portuguese colonization, the focus was on establishing coastal settlements and fortresses to facilitate the slave trade. The most significant of these was Luanda, founded in 1575 by Paulo Dias de Novais. Luanda became the administrative and commercial center of Portuguese Angola and remains the capital of the country today. The Portuguese also established other settlements, such as Benguela, which became important hubs for the export of slaves and other goods. The coastal settlements were fortified to protect against rival European powers and African resistance.

The impact of the slave trade on Angola was profound. The Portuguese and their African collaborators raided villages, capturing men, women, and children to be sold into slavery. The loss of population due to the slave trade had long-lasting demographic, social, and economic consequences. Communities were depopulated, traditional leadership structures were undermined, and social cohesion was severely disrupted. The economic focus on the slave trade also stunted the development of other economic activities, as the region became heavily dependent on the export of human beings.

Despite the devastating impact of the slave trade, the Portuguese did not establish effective control over the interior of Angola until much later. The interior regions were home to powerful African kingdoms and chiefdoms that resisted Portuguese incursions. The Kingdom of Ndongo, led by the renowned Queen Nzinga Mbande in the 17th century, is one of the most notable examples of African resistance to Portuguese colonization. Queen Nzinga, known for her diplomatic and military acumen, fought fiercely against Portuguese encroachment and sought alliances with other African states and European powers to protect her kingdom. Her resistance is emblematic of the broader struggle of African societies to maintain their sovereignty in the face of European colonization.

The formal establishment of Portuguese colonial rule in Angola began in earnest in the late 19th century, as European powers scrambled to carve up Africa during the Berlin Conference of 1884-1885. The conference formalized European claims to African territories, and Portugal was granted control over Angola. This period marked the beginning of a more intensive and systematic effort by the Portuguese to establish administrative control, exploit resources, and integrate Angola into the global capitalist economy.

The Portuguese colonial administration implemented various policies aimed at consolidating their control over Angola and exploiting its resources. One of the key aspects of Portuguese rule was the system of forced labor, known as chibalo. Africans were compelled to work on plantations, in mines, and on infrastructure projects under harsh conditions and for little or no pay. The forced labor system was justified by the colonial administration as a means of developing the colony and bringing civilization to the African population. However, it was essentially a form of exploitation that generated significant profits for the colonial economy while causing immense suffering for the African population.

Agricultural production was a major focus of Portuguese colonial policy. The colonial administration promoted the cultivation of cash crops such as coffee, cotton, and sisal, which were exported to Portugal and other international markets. Large plantations, often owned by Portuguese settlers or companies, were established, and African labor was used to cultivate and harvest the crops. The emphasis on cash crops led to the neglect of subsistence agriculture, contributing to food insecurity and economic dependency.

The discovery of significant mineral resources, particularly diamonds and oil, further intensified Portuguese exploitation of Angola. The colonial administration granted concessions to Portuguese and foreign companies to extract and export these valuable resources. The extraction of diamonds, concentrated in the northeastern regions of Angola, and oil, discovered off the coast in the 1950s, generated substantial revenue for the colonial state but did little to improve the living conditions of the African population. The wealth generated from these resources was largely siphoned off to Portugal, reinforcing the economic disparities between the colonizers and the colonized.

Portuguese colonial rule in Angola was characterized by a rigid racial hierarchy and systemic discrimination. The colonial administration implemented policies that privileged Portuguese settlers and marginalized the African population. Education, healthcare, and other social services were primarily designed to benefit the settlers, with limited provisions for Africans. The colonial government established separate schools for Europeans and Africans, with African education focused on basic literacy and vocational training intended to prepare Africans for menial jobs. The lack of access to quality education for Africans perpetuated social and economic inequalities.

The rise of nationalist movements in Africa after World War II had a significant impact on Angola. The global context of decolonization, coupled with the growing awareness of colonial injustices, fueled the emergence of nationalist movements seeking independence from Portuguese rule. The Movimento Popular de Libertação de Angola (MPLA), founded in 1956, was one of the key nationalist organizations advocating for independence. The MPLA, initially a coalition of various groups, emphasized the need for armed struggle to achieve liberation. Other significant nationalist movements included the União Nacional para a Independência Total de Angola (UNITA), founded by Jonas Savimbi in 1966, and the Frente Nacional de Libertação de Angola (FNLA), led by Holden Roberto.

The struggle for independence in Angola escalated into a protracted and brutal conflict, known as the Angolan War of Independence (1961-1974). The war was marked by guerrilla warfare, with nationalist movements launching attacks on Portuguese military and economic targets. The conflict caused immense suffering for the civilian population, with widespread displacement, casualties, and destruction of infrastructure. The Portuguese military responded with a heavy-handed approach, employing counterinsurgency tactics that included massacres, forced relocations, and the use of napalm.

The Carnation Revolution in Portugal in April 1974, a coup that overthrew the authoritarian Estado Novo regime, marked a turning point in the struggle for independence. The new Portuguese government, recognizing the untenability of maintaining colonial rule, initiated negotiations with the nationalist movements. The Alvor Agreement, signed in January 1975, set the framework for the transition to independence, including the establishment of a transitional government composed of representatives from the MPLA, UNITA, and FNLA.

However, the transition to independence was fraught with challenges and conflict. Deep-seated rivalries and ideological differences among the nationalist movements quickly escalated into a full-scale civil war. The MPLA, backed by the Soviet Union and Cuba, emerged as the dominant force and declared the establishment of the People's Republic of Angola on November 11, 1975, with Agostinho Neto as its first president. UNITA, supported by the United States and South Africa, and the FNLA, backed by Zaire, continued to challenge MPLA rule, plunging Angola into a devastating civil war that would last for decades.

The legacy of Portuguese colonization in Angola is complex and multifaceted. The colonial period left deep scars on the country's social fabric, economic structures, and political landscape. The forced labor system, land expropriation, and resource exploitation created enduring economic inequalities and social divisions. The struggle for independence and the subsequent civil war further compounded these challenges, resulting in immense human suffering and delaying the country's development.

The Portuguese language and culture have left a lasting impact on Angola, shaping its national identity and cultural landscape. Portuguese remains the official language of Angola and is widely spoken across the country. The influence of Portuguese culture is evident in various aspects of Angolan life, including literature, music, and cuisine. However, the colonial legacy also includes a sense of resilience and resistance, as the Angolan people have continually fought to assert their sovereignty and rebuild their nation in the face of adversity.

Since achieving independence, Angola has faced numerous challenges in addressing the legacies of colonialism and rebuilding its economy and society. The civil war, which officially ended in 2002, left the country with significant humanitarian and developmental challenges, including landmines, displaced populations, and destroyed infrastructure. The post-war period has seen efforts to promote national reconciliation, economic reconstruction, and political stability, but the country continues to grapple with issues such as corruption, economic inequality, and governance.

The Portuguese colonization of Angola, with its complex interplay of exploitation, resistance, and cultural exchange, remains a critical area of study for understanding the dynamics of colonialism and its long-term impacts. The history of Portuguese rule in Angola offers valuable insights into the broader patterns of European colonization in Africa, the struggles for independence, and the ongoing challenges of post-colonial development and nation-building.

Chapter 22: Danish West Indies Governance

The Danish West Indies, now known as the United States Virgin Islands, comprised the islands of Saint Thomas, Saint John, and Saint Croix. Denmark's governance of these islands, spanning nearly two centuries from the 1670s until their sale to the United States in 1917, is a complex and multifaceted chapter of colonial history. This period was characterized by economic exploitation, social stratification, and a struggle for control amidst shifting geopolitical landscapes. The Danish approach to colonial governance was marked by both continuity and change, reflecting broader trends in European imperialism.

Denmark's initial interest in the Caribbean was driven by the lucrative opportunities presented by the burgeoning sugar trade. In 1671, the Danish West India Company, a chartered company backed by the Danish crown, established its first settlement on Saint Thomas. The company's mandate was to develop the islands economically, primarily through the establishment of plantations. Saint Thomas quickly became a center for trade and commerce, with its natural harbor serving as a key hub for shipping and the transatlantic slave trade.

The governance structure of the Danish West Indies was initially shaped by the Danish West India Company, which held significant autonomy over the islands. The company's directors in Copenhagen appointed a governor to oversee the administration of the colony. This governor wielded considerable power, acting as the chief executive, military commander, and judicial authority. The governor was supported by a small bureaucracy, including officials responsible for finance, trade, and law enforcement.

Saint Thomas's economy was heavily dependent on the labor of enslaved Africans, who were forcibly brought to the island to work on the sugar plantations. The harsh conditions and brutal treatment faced by the enslaved population were characteristic of the Caribbean plantation system. Enslaved Africans were subjected to grueling labor, poor living conditions, and severe punishments. The social hierarchy was stark, with a small elite of European planters and merchants at the top, a minority of free people of color and mixed descent in the middle, and the majority enslaved African population at the bottom.

In 1718, the Danish West India Company expanded its holdings by acquiring Saint John. The island was developed along similar lines to Saint Thomas, with plantations and a reliance on slave labor. However, the rugged terrain of Saint John made large-scale plantation agriculture more challenging. Despite these difficulties, the island became an integral part of the Danish colonial economy.

The acquisition of Saint Croix in 1733 marked a significant expansion of Danish territorial claims in the Caribbean. Unlike Saint Thomas and Saint John, Saint Croix was purchased from the French West India Company. The island was larger and more fertile, making it an attractive prospect for plantation agriculture. The Danish crown took a more direct role in the administration of Saint Croix, reflecting its increased importance within the colonial economy.

Saint Croix's development was marked by the establishment of extensive sugar plantations, which relied on a large enslaved labor force. The Danish government encouraged European settlement on the island by offering land grants and other incentives to prospective planters. The island quickly became the most prosperous of the Danish West Indies, producing significant quantities of sugar, rum, and other commodities for export.

The governance of the Danish West Indies was formalized in 1754 when the Danish crown assumed direct control over the islands from the Danish West India Company. This transition reflected a broader trend in European colonial administration, where metropolitan governments sought to exert greater control over their overseas possessions. The Danish crown established a centralized administration based in Charlotte Amalie, the capital of Saint Thomas. This administration was headed by a governor-general, who oversaw the civil, military, and judicial affairs of the colony.

The governor-general was supported by a council composed of prominent planters and merchants. This council served as an advisory body and had some influence over local legislation and policy. However, ultimate authority rested with the governor-general, who reported directly to the Danish crown. The centralized nature of the administration allowed for more efficient governance and coordination of economic activities across the three islands.

The economic foundation of the Danish West Indies remained rooted in plantation agriculture and the exploitation of enslaved labor. The sugar industry dominated the colonial economy, with planters investing heavily in the cultivation of sugar cane and the production of sugar and rum. The profitability of the sugar industry was closely tied to the international market, and fluctuations in sugar prices had a significant impact on the colonial economy.

The social structure of the Danish West Indies was highly stratified. At the top of the hierarchy were the European planters and merchants, who controlled the majority of the land and wealth. Below them were the free people of color, a diverse group that included mixed-race individuals, freed slaves, and immigrants from other Caribbean islands. Despite their free status, people of color faced significant legal and social discrimination. The vast majority of the population consisted of enslaved Africans, who endured harsh conditions and had little to no rights under colonial law.

Resistance to Danish colonial rule and the institution of slavery was a constant feature of life in the Danish West Indies. Enslaved Africans resisted their oppression in various ways, from subtle forms of resistance, such as work slowdowns and sabotage, to more overt acts, including rebellion. One of the most significant slave revolts in the

Danish West Indies occurred on Saint John in 1733. Enslaved Africans, led by Akwamu leaders, seized control of the island and held it for several months before Danish and French forces reasserted control.

The abolitionist movement in Europe and the Americas gained momentum in the late 18th and early 19th centuries, leading to increased pressure on colonial powers to end the transatlantic slave trade and abolish slavery. Denmark took the significant step of abolishing the transatlantic slave trade in 1803, becoming one of the first European nations to do so. However, the institution of slavery persisted in the Danish West Indies until 1848.

The abolition of slavery in the Danish West Indies was a complex and protracted process. The enslaved population continued to resist their conditions, and pressure for emancipation grew both within the colony and from international abolitionist movements. In 1848, a large-scale slave revolt on Saint Croix, led by figures such as General Buddhoe (Moses Gottlieb), forced the Danish authorities to abolish slavery. On July 3, 1848, Governor-General Peter von Scholten issued a proclamation freeing the enslaved population.

The transition from a slave-based economy to a free labor system was fraught with challenges. The formerly enslaved population sought to establish independent livelihoods, but they faced significant obstacles, including limited access to land, credit, and economic opportunities. The colonial administration implemented labor laws designed to coerce the freed population into wage labor on the plantations, perpetuating a system of economic exploitation and inequality.

The late 19th and early 20th centuries were marked by significant changes in the governance and economy of the Danish West Indies. The decline of the sugar industry, due to competition from other sugar-producing regions and the rise of alternative sweeteners, led to economic hardship in the colony. The Danish government made efforts to diversify the economy, promoting the cultivation of other crops, such as cotton and fruit, and developing infrastructure to support trade and commerce.

Despite these efforts, the Danish West Indies continued to face economic challenges. The colonial administration struggled to balance the interests of planters, merchants, and the working population. The social and economic inequalities that had been entrenched during the era of slavery persisted, contributing to social tensions and unrest.

The geopolitical landscape of the Caribbean in the early 20th century was shaped by the strategic interests of major powers, particularly the United States. The U.S. viewed the Danish West Indies as a valuable strategic asset, given their location near the Panama Canal and key shipping routes. Negotiations between Denmark and the United States regarding the sale of the islands began in the early 20th century, influenced by the broader context of World War I and the shifting balance of power in the region.

In 1917, Denmark sold the Danish West Indies to the United States for $25 million, and the islands were renamed the United States Virgin Islands. The transfer of sovereignty marked the end of nearly two centuries of Danish colonial rule. The transition to American governance brought about significant changes in the political, economic, and social structures of the islands. The U.S. implemented reforms aimed at modernizing the economy and infrastructure, but the legacy of Danish colonialism continued to influence the development of the Virgin Islands.

The Danish West Indies' governance is a complex and multifaceted narrative of colonial exploitation, resistance, and transformation. The Danish colonial administration's efforts to develop the islands' economy through plantation agriculture and the transatlantic slave trade had profound and lasting impacts on the social and economic structures of the region. The struggle for freedom and equality by the enslaved population and their descendants is a testament to their resilience and resistance in the face of oppression.

The legacy of Danish rule in the Virgin Islands is evident in various aspects of contemporary life, including cultural traditions, language, and social dynamics. The history of the Danish West Indies offers valuable insights into the broader patterns of European colonialism in the Caribbean and the enduring legacies of colonial exploitation and resistance. The transition from Danish to American governance marked a new chapter in the islands' history, but the challenges of addressing the historical injustices and inequalities of the colonial period continue to shape the present and future of the Virgin Islands.

Chapter 23: British Influence in the Caribbean

British influence in the Caribbean is a vast and intricate subject that encompasses the colonization, administration, cultural impact, economic development, and social changes imposed by the British Empire over several centuries. The British Caribbean, consisting of islands such as Jamaica, Barbados, Trinidad and Tobago, the Bahamas, and others, has been profoundly shaped by British colonial policies and practices. This influence has left a lasting legacy that continues to affect the region's political, economic, social, and cultural landscapes today.

The British began their colonization of the Caribbean in the early 17th century, driven by the allure of profitable agricultural ventures and strategic military positioning. The initial forays into the region included the establishment of settlements on islands such as St. Kitts in 1624, Barbados in 1627, and Nevis in 1628. These early colonies quickly became important centers for sugar production, which became the backbone of the Caribbean economy and a critical component of the British Empire's wealth.

The cultivation of sugar cane required significant labor, leading to the importation of enslaved Africans through the transatlantic slave trade. The brutal and dehumanizing system of slavery became the cornerstone of the British Caribbean economy. Enslaved Africans were subjected to grueling labor conditions on plantations, facing severe punishments and minimal rights. The exploitation of African labor generated enormous profits for British planters and merchants, contributing to the economic growth of the British Empire.

The sugar industry in the British Caribbean was characterized by the establishment of large plantations owned by European settlers. These plantations were highly profitable but also extremely labor-intensive. The enslaved population, forcibly brought from Africa, outnumbered the European settlers, leading to a rigid and hierarchical social structure based on race. The planters formed the elite class, controlling the political and economic life of the colonies, while the vast majority of the population, consisting of enslaved Africans, lived in harsh and oppressive conditions.

The British colonial administration in the Caribbean was designed to maintain order, maximize economic output, and protect British interests. Each colony was governed by a British-appointed governor, who acted as the representative of the British Crown. The governor was supported by a council, often composed of local elites, and an elected assembly that included representatives of the planter class. The legislative framework was designed to enforce colonial policies and regulate the economy, particularly the lucrative sugar trade.

The economic model of the British Caribbean was heavily dependent on the triangular trade, involving the exchange of goods between Europe, Africa, and the Americas. British ships transported manufactured goods to Africa, where they were exchanged for enslaved Africans. These enslaved individuals were then shipped to the Caribbean and sold to plantation owners. The final leg of the journey involved the transportation of sugar, rum, and other colonial products back to Europe. This system of trade was instrumental in the accumulation of wealth and the expansion of the British Empire.

The social structure of the British Caribbean was marked by significant racial and class divisions. The planter elite, consisting of wealthy European landowners, held significant power and influence. Below them were the free people of color, a diverse group that included mixed-race individuals, freed slaves, and immigrants from other regions. Despite their free status, people of color faced legal and social discrimination. At the bottom of the social hierarchy were the enslaved Africans, who were subjected to the harshest conditions and denied basic human rights.

The brutal conditions of slavery and the desire for freedom led to numerous acts of resistance and rebellion among the enslaved population. One of the most significant revolts was the 1831 Baptist War in Jamaica, led by Samuel Sharpe, an enslaved Baptist preacher. This rebellion, along with other uprisings and the growing abolitionist movement in Britain, put pressure on the British government to address the issue of slavery. The Abolition of Slavery Act was passed in 1833, leading to the emancipation of enslaved individuals in the British Caribbean by 1838.

The abolition of slavery brought significant changes to the Caribbean, but it did not end the economic exploitation or social inequalities. The plantation economy continued to rely on cheap labor, leading to the importation of indentured laborers from India, China, and other regions. These laborers worked under contracts that often placed them in conditions similar to those experienced by the enslaved population. The transition from slavery to indentured labor helped sustain the sugar industry, but it also introduced new cultural and social dynamics to the Caribbean.

The late 19th and early 20th centuries were marked by significant economic and social transformations in the British Caribbean. The decline of the sugar industry, due to competition from other sugar-producing regions and the development of alternative sweeteners, led to economic challenges. The colonial governments attempted to diversify the economy by promoting the cultivation of other crops, such as bananas and cocoa, and developing tourism as a new source of revenue. Despite these efforts, the Caribbean economies remained vulnerable to global market fluctuations and dependent on foreign investment.

The early 20th century also saw the rise of nationalist movements and demands for political reform in the British Caribbean. Inspired by global movements for decolonization and self-determination, Caribbean leaders began to push for greater autonomy and representation. The labor unrest of the 1930s, driven by poor working conditions, economic hardship, and social inequalities, played a crucial role in shaping the political landscape. Strikes, protests, and the formation of labor unions highlighted the need for political change and laid the groundwork for future independence movements.

The post-World War II period marked a significant shift in the political trajectory of the British Caribbean. The war had highlighted the strategic importance of the region and the contributions of Caribbean soldiers to the Allied war effort. This period also saw increased pressure for decolonization and self-governance. The British government began to implement political reforms, granting limited self-government to some colonies and increasing representation in colonial legislatures.

The 1960s and 1970s were a period of rapid decolonization in the British Caribbean. Several territories achieved independence, starting with Jamaica and Trinidad and Tobago in 1962. Barbados followed in 1966, and other islands, including the Bahamas, Grenada, and Saint Vincent and the Grenadines, gained independence in subsequent years. The process of decolonization was marked by the establishment of democratic institutions, the development of national identities, and the pursuit of economic diversification and social development.

Despite achieving political independence, the newly formed Caribbean nations faced significant challenges. The legacy of colonialism, including economic dependency, social inequalities, and political instability, continued to shape their development. Many Caribbean countries struggled with issues such as poverty, unemployment, and inadequate infrastructure. The global economic system, dominated by former colonial powers and multinational corporations, further complicated efforts to achieve sustainable development and economic self-sufficiency.

British cultural influence in the Caribbean has been profound and enduring. The English language, legal systems, educational institutions, and cultural practices established during the colonial period continue to play a central role in Caribbean societies. The British Caribbean has produced a rich cultural heritage, including literature, music, and art, that reflects the region's diverse history and experiences. Notable Caribbean writers, such as V.S. Naipaul, Derek Walcott, and Jamaica Kincaid, have gained international recognition for their contributions to literature, exploring themes of identity, colonialism, and postcolonialism.

The British influence on Caribbean music is also significant. Genres such as reggae, calypso, and dancehall have their roots in the cultural exchanges and social conditions of the colonial and postcolonial periods. These musical forms have become powerful expressions of Caribbean identity and resistance, gaining global popularity and influencing other musical traditions. The cultural dynamism of the Caribbean is a testament to the resilience and creativity of its people, who have navigated and transcended the challenges of colonialism and its aftermath.

In contemporary times, the relationship between the Caribbean and the United Kingdom remains complex. Many Caribbean nations maintain close ties with Britain through the Commonwealth, an organization of former British colonies. These ties include political, economic, and cultural connections, as well as the ongoing movement of people between the Caribbean and the UK. The Caribbean diaspora in the UK has played a crucial role in shaping British society, contributing to its cultural diversity and participating in various aspects of public life.

The history of British influence in the Caribbean is a multifaceted narrative of exploitation, resistance, adaptation, and transformation. The colonial period left deep and lasting impacts on the region's political, economic, social, and cultural landscapes. The struggle for independence and the postcolonial challenges highlights the resilience and agency of Caribbean peoples in shaping their own destinies. The enduring legacies of British colonialism continue to influence the Caribbean, but the region has also forged its own path, drawing on its rich heritage and diverse experiences to navigate the complexities of the modern world.

Chapter 24: French Rule in Madagascar

French rule in Madagascar represents a significant chapter in the island's history, marked by colonization, resistance, economic exploitation, and cultural transformation. This period, spanning from the late 19th century until Madagascar's independence in 1960, left a profound and lasting impact on the island's political, social, and economic landscapes. Understanding this era requires a detailed examination of the events leading up to French colonization, the methods of administration, the economic strategies employed by the French, the resistance movements that emerged, and the enduring legacies of French rule.

The roots of French interest in Madagascar can be traced back to the early 17th century when French traders and missionaries began to establish a presence on the island. However, it was not until the late 19th century that France made a concerted effort to colonize Madagascar. The island's strategic location in the Indian Ocean, coupled with its potential for agricultural and mineral exploitation, made it an attractive target for French imperial ambitions. In 1883, the French launched the first Franco-Hova War against the Merina Kingdom, which controlled much of the island. The war resulted in a French victory and the imposition of a protectorate over Madagascar in 1885.

The establishment of the protectorate marked the beginning of formal French rule, but it was not until 1896, following the second Franco-Hova War, that Madagascar was officially annexed as a French colony. General Joseph Gallieni, appointed as the first Governor-General of Madagascar, played a crucial role in consolidating French control over the island. Gallieni implemented a policy of "pacification," which involved the systematic suppression of resistance and the establishment of French authority throughout the island. This often brutal campaign included military expeditions, the destruction of villages, and the execution of rebel leaders.

The French administration in Madagascar was characterized by a highly centralized and authoritarian system of governance. The island was divided into administrative regions, each overseen by a French official. Traditional Malagasy political structures were dismantled, and the authority of local chiefs was subordinated to the colonial administration. The French implemented a system of forced labor, known as "corvée," which required Malagasy people to work on public projects, such as roads, railways, and plantations. This system was deeply resented by the local population and contributed to widespread unrest and resistance.

Economically, the French sought to transform Madagascar into a profitable colony that could supply raw materials for French industries and serve as a market for French goods. The colonial administration promoted the cultivation of cash crops, such as coffee, vanilla, and sisal, which were exported to Europe. French settlers were encouraged to establish plantations, and large tracts of land were expropriated from Malagasy communities. The emphasis on cash crop agriculture disrupted traditional farming practices and contributed to food insecurity among the local population.

The exploitation of Madagascar's natural resources extended beyond agriculture. The French developed mining operations to extract valuable minerals, such as graphite, mica, and chromite. Infrastructure projects, including the construction of railways and ports, facilitated the extraction and export of these resources. However, the benefits of this economic activity were largely concentrated in the hands of the French colonizers and a small elite of Malagasy collaborators, while the majority of the population experienced little improvement in their living standards.

The imposition of French cultural and educational policies was another significant aspect of colonial rule in Madagascar. The French sought to assimilate the Malagasy population by promoting the French language and culture. French became the language of administration, education, and commerce, and efforts were made to suppress the use of Malagasy languages. French-style schools were established to educate the Malagasy elite, who were expected to adopt French cultural norms and values. This policy of assimilation aimed to create a class of loyal, Westernized Malagasy who would support the colonial regime.

Despite these efforts, resistance to French rule persisted throughout the colonial period. The initial military campaigns of pacification did not entirely eliminate opposition, and periodic uprisings and rebellions continued to challenge French authority. One of the most significant resistance movements emerged in the early 20th century, known as the Menalamba Rebellion. The Menalamba, or "Red Shawl" movement, consisted of rural Malagasy who opposed the imposition of French rule and the disruption of traditional ways of life. The rebellion was eventually suppressed, but it highlighted the deep-seated resentment and resistance among the Malagasy population.

The struggle for independence gained momentum after World War II, as nationalist movements across Africa and Asia sought to end colonial rule. In Madagascar, the Malagasy Uprising of 1947 was a pivotal moment in the fight for independence. The uprising began as a coordinated attack by nationalist groups against French colonial authorities and settlers. The French response was swift and brutal, involving widespread reprisals, mass arrests, and the execution of suspected rebels. Estimates of the number of Malagasy killed during the suppression of the uprising range from tens of thousands to over a hundred thousand. The brutality of the French response drew international condemnation and increased support for the independence movement.

The post-war period saw significant political changes in Madagascar. In 1956, the French government introduced the Loi

Cadre, which granted a degree of self-government to its African colonies, including Madagascar. This law allowed for the establishment of local assemblies and increased political participation for Malagasy citizens. Political parties emerged, and nationalist leaders began to push for full independence. In 1958, a referendum was held in Madagascar, and the majority of voters chose to become an autonomous republic within the French Community. Finally, on June 26, 1960, Madagascar achieved full independence from France.

The legacy of French rule in Madagascar is complex and multifaceted. The colonial period left a lasting impact on the island's political, economic, and social structures. The centralized and authoritarian nature of colonial governance influenced the post-independence political landscape, where power was often concentrated in the hands of a few elites. The economic policies of the colonial era, focused on cash crops and resource extraction, continued to shape the Malagasy economy, contributing to ongoing challenges of poverty and underdevelopment.

Culturally, the influence of French rule is evident in the continued use of the French language, particularly in education, government, and business. French cultural practices, such as cuisine, fashion, and religion, have also left their mark on Malagasy society. However, the colonial period also fostered a strong sense of national identity and pride in Malagasy culture, which has been a source of resilience and resistance against external influences.

The memory of resistance to French rule is an important aspect of Madagascar's national consciousness. Figures like Ranavalona III, the last queen of Madagascar, and nationalist leaders like Philibert Tsiranana, who became the first president of independent Madagascar, are celebrated as symbols of the struggle for freedom and self-determination. The commemoration of the Malagasy Uprising of 1947 serves as a reminder of the sacrifices made in the fight for independence and the enduring desire for sovereignty and dignity.

In contemporary Madagascar, the relationship with France remains significant, characterized by both cooperation and tension. Economic ties between the two countries continue, with France being a major trading partner and source of investment. Development aid and cultural exchanges also play a role in maintaining connections between Madagascar and its former colonial power. However, the legacy of colonialism, including issues of economic inequality, political instability, and cultural hegemony, continues to influence the dynamics of this relationship.

French rule in Madagascar was a period of profound transformation, marked by conquest, exploitation, resistance, and the eventual achievement of independence. The colonial legacy has left deep and lasting imprints on the island's political, economic, and cultural landscapes. Understanding this history is essential for appreciating the complexities of contemporary Madagascar and the ongoing challenges and opportunities faced by its people. The resilience and strength demonstrated by the Malagasy in the face of colonial oppression remain a powerful testament to their enduring spirit and determination to shape their own destiny.

Chapter 25: Italian Occupation of Eritrea

The Italian occupation of Eritrea is a significant historical period that began in the late 19th century and extended into the mid-20th century. This period was marked by Italy's ambitions to establish a colonial empire in East Africa, the impact of Italian colonial policies on Eritrea's social, economic, and political structures, and the complex legacies of Italian rule that continue to influence Eritrea today.

The roots of Italian interest in Eritrea can be traced back to the late 19th century when European powers were engaged in the so-called "Scramble for Africa." Italy, a relatively new nation-state unified in 1861, sought to assert itself as a colonial power. In 1882, Italy purchased the port of Assab from the local sultan, marking the beginning of its colonial presence in the region. This acquisition was part of a broader strategy to establish a foothold in the strategically important Red Sea area, which was a vital maritime route for trade and military purposes.

Italy's colonial ambitions in Eritrea were solidified with the signing of the Treaty of Wuchale in 1889 between Italy and Emperor Menelik II of Ethiopia. The treaty, however, contained discrepancies in its Italian and Amharic versions, leading to differing interpretations regarding the nature of Italian sovereignty. The Italians believed the treaty granted them a protectorate over Ethiopia, while Menelik II viewed it as a treaty of friendship and commerce. This misunderstanding eventually led to the Battle of Adwa in 1896, where Ethiopian forces decisively defeated the Italian army, curbing Italian expansion into Ethiopia but leaving Eritrea firmly under Italian control.

The formal establishment of Eritrea as an Italian colony occurred in 1890. The Italian colonial administration began to develop the infrastructure and economy of the colony, focusing on building roads, railways, and ports to facilitate trade and military movements. The capital, Asmara, was transformed from a small village into a bustling city with European-style architecture, modern amenities, and a diverse population of Italians and Eritreans.

The Italian colonial policies in Eritrea were characterized by a combination of economic exploitation and attempts to integrate Eritrea into the broader Italian empire. The Italians introduced large-scale agricultural projects, including the cultivation of cotton, coffee, and other cash crops. These projects often involved the expropriation of land from local communities and the imposition of forced labor, creating tensions between the colonizers and the indigenous population. Additionally, Italian settlers were encouraged to move to Eritrea, leading to the establishment of Italian-run farms, businesses, and industries.

The colonial administration also implemented policies aimed at assimilating the Eritrean population into Italian culture and society. Italian became the language of administration, education, and commerce, and efforts were made to promote Italian cultural norms and values. Schools were established to educate Eritrean children in the Italian language and curriculum, and many Eritreans converted to Roman Catholicism, although traditional religions and Islam remained prevalent.

Despite these assimilation efforts, Eritrean society retained a strong sense of identity and resistance to colonial rule. The Italians faced various forms of resistance, ranging from passive non-compliance to active rebellion. One notable figure in the resistance movement was Hamid Idris Awate, who would later become a prominent leader in the fight for Eritrean independence. The Italian administration responded to resistance with repression, employing military force and punitive measures to maintain control.

The Italian occupation of Eritrea was disrupted by World War II. In 1941, British and Allied forces launched a military campaign against Italian East Africa, resulting in the defeat of Italian forces and the end of Italian colonial rule in Eritrea. Eritrea was placed under British military administration, marking the beginning of a transitional period that would eventually lead to Eritrea's federation with Ethiopia in 1952 and its subsequent struggle for independence.

The legacy of Italian colonialism in Eritrea is multifaceted and complex. On one hand, the Italians introduced modern infrastructure, education, and health care systems that contributed to the development of the colony. The city of Asmara, in particular, is often cited as a legacy of Italian urban planning and architecture, with its well-preserved Art Deco buildings and European-style streetscapes.

On the other hand, Italian colonial rule was marked by exploitation, repression, and social disruption. The imposition of forced labor, land expropriation, and economic policies designed to benefit the colonizers often resulted in hardship and resentment among the Eritrean population. The cultural assimilation policies also had a lasting impact, creating a legacy of linguistic and cultural influence that persists in Eritrea today.

The period of Italian rule also contributed to the development of a distinct Eritrean national identity. The shared experience of colonization, resistance, and the struggle for independence fostered a sense of unity and solidarity among Eritreans. This national consciousness would later play a crucial role in the Eritrean liberation movement, which ultimately achieved independence from Ethiopia in 1993.

In contemporary Eritrea, the legacy of Italian colonialism is evident in various aspects of society. The Italian language continues to be taught in schools, and many Eritreans, particularly those in older generations, speak Italian fluently. Italian cultural influences can be seen in Eritrean cuisine, fashion, and everyday life. The architectural heritage of Asmara, with its Italian-designed buildings and urban layout, remains a source of pride and a symbol of Eritrea's unique history.

The Italian period also left a lasting impact on Eritrea's political and economic structures. The centralized and authoritarian nature of colonial governance influenced the post-independence political landscape, where power has often been concentrated in the hands of a few elites. The economic policies of the colonial era, focused on cash crops and resource extraction, contributed to ongoing challenges of poverty and underdevelopment in the post-independence period.

The history of Italian occupation in Eritrea is a complex narrative of conquest, colonization, resistance, and transformation. The period left deep and lasting imprints on Eritrea's political, economic, and cultural landscapes, shaping the island's development and identity. Understanding this history is essential for appreciating the complexities of contemporary Eritrea and the ongoing challenges and opportunities faced by its people. The resilience and strength demonstrated by Eritreans in the face of colonial oppression remain a powerful testament to their enduring spirit and determination to shape their own destiny.

Chapter 26: German Colonization of Tanzania

The German colonization of Tanzania, then known as German East Africa, is a significant chapter in the history of the region. This period, spanning from the late 19th century to the end of World War I, had a profound and lasting impact on the political, social, and economic landscape of Tanzania. German East Africa included the present-day territories of mainland Tanzania, Rwanda, and Burundi. The colonization process involved complex interactions between the German colonial administration and the diverse ethnic groups inhabiting the region, characterized by conquest, resistance, exploitation, and efforts to modernize the colony.

The origins of German involvement in East Africa can be traced back to the Berlin Conference of 1884-1885, where European powers convened to divide Africa into spheres of influence. Germany, a relatively new nation-state unified in 1871, sought to assert itself as a colonial power. Under the leadership of Chancellor Otto von Bismarck, Germany acquired several colonies in Africa, including what would become German East Africa. The initial foothold in the region was established through the activities of the German East Africa Company, a private enterprise chartered by the German government to facilitate trade and exploration.

The first significant step towards formal colonization occurred in 1885 when Carl Peters, a representative of the German East Africa Company, signed treaties with several local chiefs, ostensibly placing their territories under German protection. These treaties, often obtained through deception or coercion, laid the groundwork for German claims to the region. The company's activities soon led to conflicts with both local African rulers and the Sultan of Zanzibar, who nominally controlled the coastal areas.

In 1888, the German government took direct control of the region, establishing the colony of German East Africa. The transition from company rule to direct colonial administration was marked by the Abushiri Revolt, a significant uprising led by the coastal Arab and Swahili populations against German authority. The revolt, driven by grievances over German interference in local trade and administration, was suppressed with considerable brutality. German military expeditions, led by officers such as Hermann Wissmann, crushed the resistance, securing German control over the coastal areas and paving the way for further inland expansion.

The consolidation of German rule involved the establishment of a centralized and authoritarian administration. The colony was divided into administrative districts, each overseen by a German official known as a Bezirksamtmann. These officials wielded considerable power, often operating with little oversight from the colonial capital in Dar es Salaam. The administration relied heavily on military force to maintain order and suppress resistance, employing African soldiers, known as askaris, in the Schutztruppe (colonial troops).

Economically, the German colonial administration sought to transform German East Africa into a profitable enterprise that could supply raw materials for German industries and serve as a market for German goods. The colonial economy was characterized by the promotion of large-scale agriculture, particularly the cultivation of cash crops such as sisal, cotton, and coffee. European settlers were encouraged to establish plantations, often on land expropriated from African communities. The German administration also invested in infrastructure projects, including the construction of railways and ports, to facilitate the export of agricultural products and minerals.

One of the most significant infrastructure projects was the construction of the Central Line Railway, which connected the coastal city of Dar es Salaam to the interior regions of the colony. The railway facilitated the movement of goods and people, but it also disrupted traditional trade routes and patterns of settlement. The forced labor policies, known as the kipande system, were implemented to ensure a steady supply of labor for these projects. Africans were required to carry identification passes and were often conscripted into labor gangs under harsh conditions.

The imposition of German rule and the economic exploitation of the colony led to significant social and cultural changes. The Germans sought to impose their language, culture, and administrative practices on the local population. Missionary activities were encouraged, and Christian missions established schools, clinics, and churches throughout the colony. These missions played a dual role in providing social services and promoting the assimilation of African communities into European cultural norms.

Resistance to German rule was a constant feature of the colonial period. The most notable and widespread resistance movement was the Maji Maji Rebellion of 1905-1907. The rebellion was sparked by grievances over forced labor, taxation, and the alienation of land for European plantations. The movement, named after the belief in a sacred water (maji) that would protect fighters from bullets, united various ethnic groups in a concerted effort to expel the Germans. The rebellion was met with a brutal response from the German military, resulting in the deaths of an estimated 75,000 to 300,000 Africans due to warfare, famine, and disease. The suppression of the Maji Maji Rebellion marked a turning point in German colonial policy, leading to some reforms and a reduction in the use of forced labor.

The impact of German colonization on the social structures of East African societies was profound. Traditional systems of governance were disrupted, and the authority of local chiefs and elders was undermined by the imposition of colonial rule. The introduction of European legal and administrative systems created new social hierarchies and power dynamics. The missionary activities, while providing education and healthcare, also contributed to the erosion of indigenous cultural practices and beliefs.

World War I had a significant impact on German East Africa. The colony became a major theater of conflict, with British, Belgian, and Portuguese forces launching a coordinated campaign to seize control from the Germans. Under the leadership of General Paul von Lettow-Vorbeck, the German Schutztruppe waged a protracted guerrilla war, employing hit-and-run tactics and relying on local support. Despite being outnumbered and outgunned, Lettow-Vorbeck's forces managed to hold out until the end of the war in 1918, making him one of the few German commanders to remain undefeated.

The end of World War I marked the end of German colonial rule in East Africa. Under the Treaty of Versailles, German East Africa was divided among the victorious Allied powers. The majority of the territory, including present-day Tanzania, was transferred to British control, becoming the mandate of Tanganyika. The regions corresponding to modern-day Rwanda and Burundi were assigned to Belgium. The transition to British rule brought significant changes to the administration and policies of the colony, but many of the structures and systems established during the German period remained in place.

The legacy of German colonization in Tanzania is complex and multifaceted. On one hand, the Germans introduced modern infrastructure, including roads, railways, and ports, which facilitated economic development. The establishment of cash crop agriculture laid the foundation for the country's future agricultural economy. The missionary schools and clinics contributed to improvements in education and healthcare, albeit within the framework of European cultural assimilation.

On the other hand, the period of German rule was marked by exploitation, repression, and social disruption. The forced labor policies, land expropriations, and brutal suppression of resistance movements left a legacy of suffering and resentment among the local population. The imposition of European legal and administrative systems disrupted traditional governance structures and contributed to the erosion of indigenous cultural practices.

The impact of German colonization continues to be felt in contemporary Tanzania. The infrastructure and economic policies introduced during the colonial period laid the groundwork for the country's development, but also created patterns of dependency and inequality that persist to this day. The social and cultural changes brought about by missionary activities and colonial policies have left a lasting imprint on Tanzanian society, influencing everything from language and education to religion and social norms.

The memory of resistance to German rule is an important aspect of Tanzanian national consciousness. Figures like Chief Mkwawa, who led resistance against German forces in the late 19th century, and the leaders of the Maji Maji Rebellion are celebrated as national heroes. The commemoration of these resistance movements serves as a reminder of the country's struggle for sovereignty and the enduring desire for self-determination.

In contemporary Tanzania, the relationship with Germany is characterized by both cooperation and reflection on the colonial past. Germany has provided development aid and support for various projects in Tanzania, including infrastructure development, healthcare, and education. There have also been efforts to address the historical injustices of the colonial period, including the repatriation of cultural artifacts and the recognition of the atrocities committed during the Maji Maji Rebellion.

The German colonization of Tanzania was a period of significant transformation, marked by conquest, exploitation, resistance, and the eventual transition to British rule. The legacy of this period continues to shape Tanzania's political, economic, and social landscape, influencing the country's development and its relationship with the wider world. Understanding this history is essential for appreciating the complexities of contemporary Tanzania and the ongoing challenges and opportunities faced by its people. The resilience and strength demonstrated by Tanzanians in the face of colonial oppression remain a powerful testament to their enduring spirit and determination to shape their own destiny.

Chapter 27: Belgian Rule in Rwanda

The Belgian rule in Rwanda is a pivotal and complex chapter in the country's history, characterized by significant social, political, and economic changes that have had long-lasting effects on the Rwandan people. This period, spanning from the end of World War I until Rwanda's independence in 1962, was marked by the imposition of colonial policies that deepened ethnic divisions, altered traditional power structures, and laid the groundwork for future conflicts, including the devastating genocide of 1994.

Belgian involvement in Rwanda began in the aftermath of World War I when the League of Nations granted Belgium a mandate to administer the former German colony of Ruanda-Urundi, which included present-day Rwanda and Burundi. Germany had lost its colonial territories following its defeat in the war, and Belgium, which had already established a colonial presence in neighboring Congo (then the Belgian Congo), was given the responsibility of governing these territories. The mandate system required Belgium to prepare the territories for eventual self-governance, but in practice, it led to the establishment of a new colonial regime.

Belgium's approach to colonial administration in Rwanda was significantly different from that of the Germans. The Belgians sought to exert tighter control over the territory and implemented a system of indirect rule, relying on the existing Tutsi monarchy and chiefs to administer the colony on their behalf. The Belgian authorities codified and reinforced the social hierarchy that placed the Tutsi minority in positions of power over the Hutu majority and the Twa, a smaller ethnic group. This system was rooted in a racial ideology that falsely portrayed the Tutsi as inherently superior to the Hutu and Twa, based on pseudo-scientific theories of racial difference.

One of the first major changes implemented by the Belgian administration was the introduction of identity cards in the 1930s, which classified Rwandans as Tutsi, Hutu, or Twa. This formalized and institutionalized ethnic divisions that had previously been more fluid and based on social and economic status rather than rigid racial categories. The identity cards exacerbated tensions between the ethnic groups, as the Tutsi were favored for administrative positions, education, and economic opportunities, while the Hutu and Twa were marginalized.

The Belgian authorities also undertook significant changes in the realm of agriculture and land use. They promoted the cultivation of cash crops, such as coffee and tea, to generate revenue for the colonial administration. This shift from subsistence farming to cash crop agriculture disrupted traditional agricultural practices and increased the dependency of the rural population on the colonial economy. The introduction of forced labor, known as corvée, required Rwandans to work on infrastructure projects and European-owned plantations, further straining relations between the colonizers and the indigenous population.

Education was another area where Belgian colonial policies had a profound impact. Missionary schools, primarily run by Catholic missions, became the main providers of education in Rwanda. These schools often favored Tutsi students, who were seen as the natural leaders of the country, over Hutu and Twa students. The education system reinforced the existing social hierarchy and created a small, educated elite that was predominantly Tutsi. This elite was groomed for administrative roles within the colonial government, while the majority of Hutu and Twa remained excluded from opportunities for upward mobility.

Religion also played a significant role in Belgian colonial policy. The Catholic Church became a powerful ally of the colonial administration, and Catholicism spread rapidly throughout Rwanda. The church's influence extended into the realms of education, healthcare, and social services, further entrenching its position in

Rwandan society. The alliance between the church and the colonial authorities reinforced the social and political dominance of the Tutsi elite, who were often converts to Catholicism.

Despite the apparent stability of Belgian rule, underlying tensions between the ethnic groups continued to simmer. The favoritism shown to the Tutsi elite and the marginalization of the Hutu majority created a sense of grievance and resentment among the Hutu population. The rigid ethnic classifications imposed by the identity cards and the unequal distribution of resources and opportunities deepened these divisions.

The period after World War II saw increased political activity and demands for independence across Africa, and Rwanda was no exception. The Hutu began to organize politically, demanding greater representation and an end to Tutsi domination. In response to these pressures, the Belgian authorities began to shift their support from the Tutsi elite to the Hutu majority, recognizing the need to address the growing demands for political and social reform. This shift culminated in the 1959 Hutu Revolution, also known as the Social Revolution or the "Wind of Destruction."

The Hutu Revolution was a turning point in Rwandan history. Sparked by the assassination of a Hutu sub-chief, the revolution saw widespread violence against the Tutsi population, leading to the deaths of thousands and the displacement of many more. The Tutsi monarchy was overthrown, and the Belgian administration, now supporting the Hutu majority, facilitated the establishment of a republican government dominated by Hutu politicians. This marked the end of centuries of Tutsi dominance and the beginning of a new era of Hutu rule.

In 1961, Rwanda held a referendum in which the majority of the population voted to abolish the monarchy and establish a republic. The following year, Rwanda gained its independence from Belgium on July 1, 1962. The first president of independent Rwanda was Grégoire

Kayibanda, a Hutu leader who had played a key role in the Hutu Revolution. Independence brought new challenges, as the deep-seated ethnic divisions and resentments that had been exacerbated by colonial rule continued to shape the political landscape of the new nation.

The legacy of Belgian rule in Rwanda is complex and multifaceted. On one hand, the Belgians introduced modern infrastructure, education, and healthcare systems that contributed to the development of the colony. The promotion of cash crop agriculture and the construction of roads and railways facilitated economic growth. The spread of Catholicism brought new social services and educational opportunities, albeit within a framework that reinforced existing social hierarchies.

On the other hand, Belgian colonial policies had deeply divisive effects on Rwandan society. The rigid ethnic classifications, the favoritism shown to the Tutsi elite, and the marginalization of the Hutu majority created a legacy of ethnic tension and conflict. The introduction of forced labor and the disruption of traditional agricultural practices contributed to economic hardship and social unrest. The education system, while providing opportunities for some, reinforced social divisions and created a small elite that was disconnected from the broader population.

The impact of Belgian rule continued to be felt long after independence. The deep-seated ethnic divisions and grievances that had been exacerbated by colonial policies played a significant role in the political instability and violence that plagued Rwanda in the decades following independence. The most tragic manifestation of these tensions was the Rwandan Genocide of 1994, in which an estimated 800,000 Tutsi and moderate Hutu were killed by extremist Hutu militias in a horrific campaign of ethnic cleansing.

The genocide was the result of a complex interplay of historical, political, and social factors, but the legacies of colonial rule, including the deep-seated ethnic divisions and the concentration of power and resources in the hands of a small elite, played a significant role in creating the conditions for such a catastrophe. The genocide left a deep scar on Rwandan society and prompted a period of intense reflection and reconciliation in the years that followed.

In contemporary Rwanda, efforts to address the legacies of colonial rule and the trauma of the genocide have been central to the country's development. The government, led by President Paul Kagame since 2000, has focused on promoting national unity and reconciliation, reducing ethnic divisions, and fostering economic growth and development. The promotion of education, healthcare, and infrastructure development has been a key priority, as has the effort to create a more inclusive and equitable society.

The relationship between Rwanda and Belgium has also evolved in the post-colonial period. Belgium has provided development aid and support for various projects in Rwanda, including initiatives aimed at promoting reconciliation and economic development. There have been efforts to address the historical injustices of the colonial period, including the return of cultural artifacts and the recognition of the impact of colonial policies on Rwandan society.

The Belgian rule in Rwanda was a period of significant transformation and upheaval. The policies implemented by the colonial administration had profound and lasting effects on the political, social, and economic landscape of the country. Understanding this history is essential for appreciating the complexities of contemporary Rwanda and the ongoing challenges and opportunities faced by its people. The resilience and strength demonstrated by Rwandans in the face of colonial oppression and the subsequent struggle for independence and reconciliation remain a powerful testament to their enduring spirit and determination to shape their own destiny.

Chapter 28: Japanese Expansion into Manchuria

Japanese expansion into Manchuria, also known as the Manchurian Incident or the Mukden Incident, is a significant and complex chapter in East Asian history that played a crucial role in shaping the geopolitical landscape of the region in the early 20th century. This period, which spans from the early 1900s to the end of World War II, is marked by Japan's imperial ambitions, the subsequent establishment of the puppet state of Manchukuo, and the long-lasting repercussions for China, Japan, and the broader international community.

The roots of Japanese interest in Manchuria can be traced back to the late 19th century, during a time when Japan was rapidly modernizing and seeking to assert itself as a major world power. Following the Meiji Restoration in 1868, Japan embarked on a path of industrialization, military expansion, and imperialism. The Sino-Japanese War of 1894-1895 and the Russo-Japanese War of 1904-1905 were key conflicts that demonstrated Japan's growing military capabilities and its ambitions in East Asia. The Treaty of Portsmouth, which ended the Russo-Japanese War, granted Japan control over the South Manchurian Railway and significant influence in the region, further fueling its interest in Manchuria.

Manchuria, a resource-rich region located in northeastern China, was of strategic and economic importance to Japan. It offered abundant natural resources, including coal, iron, and agricultural products, which were essential for Japan's industrial economy. Additionally, Manchuria's geographical location provided a strategic buffer zone against Russia and a potential launchpad for further expansion into China and beyond. The Japanese government and military, particularly the influential Kwantung Army, saw the control of Manchuria as vital to Japan's national security and economic interests.

The turning point in Japan's expansion into Manchuria came on September 18, 1931, with the Mukden Incident. On this day, a section of the South Manchurian Railway near Mukden (modern-day Shenyang) was blown up. Although the explosion caused only minor damage, the Japanese Kwantung Army used it as a pretext to launch a full-scale invasion of Manchuria. The explosion was later revealed to have been orchestrated by the Kwantung Army itself as a false flag operation to justify the invasion. Within a few months, Japanese forces had occupied the entire region, facing minimal resistance from the Chinese military.

The invasion of Manchuria and the subsequent establishment of the puppet state of Manchukuo in 1932 marked a significant escalation in Japanese imperial ambitions. The Kwantung Army installed Puyi, the last emperor of the Qing Dynasty, as the nominal ruler of Manchukuo, though real power remained firmly in Japanese hands. Manchukuo was presented to the world as an independent state, but it was, in reality, a puppet regime controlled by Japan. The creation of Manchukuo allowed Japan to exploit the region's resources and establish a strategic military presence.

The international response to Japan's actions in Manchuria was one of condemnation, but it was largely ineffective in curbing Japanese aggression. The League of Nations, the international organization established to maintain peace and resolve conflicts, conducted an investigation and concluded that Japan had acted unlawfully. In response, Japan withdrew from the League of Nations in 1933, demonstrating its willingness to defy international opinion and pursue its expansionist policies unilaterally. The failure of the League of Nations to take decisive action against Japan highlighted the weaknesses of the organization and emboldened other aggressive powers, such as Nazi Germany and Fascist Italy.

The occupation of Manchuria and the establishment of Manchukuo had profound and far-reaching consequences for the region and the world. In Manchuria, Japanese rule brought about significant changes in the economic, social, and political landscape. The Japanese invested heavily in infrastructure, including the construction of railways, roads, and industrial facilities. These developments were aimed at exploiting Manchuria's resources and integrating the region into the Japanese empire's economic system. The Japanese also implemented policies to attract settlers from Japan, Korea, and Taiwan to colonize Manchuria, creating a multi-ethnic society under Japanese control.

Despite the economic development, Japanese rule in Manchuria was marked by repression and exploitation. The local Chinese population faced discrimination and harsh treatment, and any resistance to Japanese rule was met with brutal suppression. The establishment of Manchukuo also exacerbated tensions between Japan and China, contributing to the broader conflict between the two nations. The Chinese government, led by the Nationalist Party (Kuomintang) under Chiang Kai-shek, refused to recognize Manchukuo and continued to resist Japanese expansion.

The occupation of Manchuria was a prelude to the broader conflict between Japan and China, known as the Second Sino-Japanese War, which began in 1937. This war saw widespread atrocities committed by Japanese forces, including the infamous Nanjing Massacre, where hundreds of thousands of Chinese civilians and disarmed soldiers were killed. The conflict further strained Japan's relations with the international community and set the stage for its involvement in World War II.

During World War II, Manchuria remained a crucial base for Japanese military operations in Asia. The region's resources and industrial capacity were vital to Japan's war effort. However, as the tide of the war turned against Japan, Manchuria became a target for Allied forces. In August 1945, the Soviet Union, honoring its commitment to the Allies, invaded Manchuria in a massive military operation. The

Soviet invasion, combined with the atomic bombings of Hiroshima and Nagasaki, forced Japan to surrender, bringing an end to World War II.

The end of the war and the subsequent surrender of Japan marked the end of Japanese rule in Manchuria. The region was placed under Soviet occupation, and the puppet state of Manchukuo was dissolved. The Soviet Union facilitated the transfer of power to Chinese Communist forces, who were engaged in a civil war against the Nationalists. By 1949, the Chinese Communist Party, led by Mao Zedong, had emerged victorious, and Manchuria became an integral part of the newly established People's Republic of China.

The legacy of Japanese expansion into Manchuria is complex and multifaceted. The period of Japanese rule left a lasting impact on the region's economic development, infrastructure, and social structure. The industrialization and infrastructure projects initiated by the Japanese laid the foundation for Manchuria's post-war economic growth. However, the period was also marked by exploitation, repression, and significant human suffering. The actions of the Japanese military and the establishment of Manchukuo contributed to the deep-seated animosities and historical grievances between China and Japan, which continue to influence relations between the two countries to this day.

The memory of Japanese expansion into Manchuria is a contentious issue in both Chinese and Japanese societies. In China, the period is remembered as a time of suffering and resistance, and the atrocities committed by Japanese forces are commemorated in numerous memorials and museums. In Japan, the legacy of the period is more complex, with debates over historical memory, responsibility, and the portrayal of the past. The events in Manchuria remain a sensitive topic in Sino-Japanese relations, influencing diplomatic interactions and regional politics.

The international community also continues to grapple with the legacy of Japanese expansion into Manchuria. The failure of the League of Nations to effectively address Japanese aggression is often cited as a cautionary tale about the limitations of international organizations and the challenges of collective security. The period serves as a reminder of the importance of addressing grievances, promoting reconciliation, and fostering a shared understanding of history to prevent future conflicts.

Chapter 29: Spanish Colonization of Florida

The Spanish colonization of Florida represents a significant chapter in the history of European exploration and settlement in the New World. This period, spanning from the early 16th century to the late 18th century, is characterized by a series of expeditions, the establishment of settlements, interactions with Indigenous peoples, military conflicts, and economic endeavors. The Spanish efforts to colonize Florida were driven by a combination of strategic, economic, and religious motives, and their legacy continues to influence the region's cultural and historical landscape.

The story of Spanish colonization in Florida begins with the voyage of Juan Ponce de León, a Spanish explorer who is traditionally credited with the discovery of Florida in 1513. Ponce de León, who had previously served as the governor of Puerto Rico, embarked on an expedition to find new lands and, according to legend, the mythical Fountain of Youth. On April 2, 1513, he sighted the coast of Florida, near what is now St. Augustine, and named the land "La Florida" (meaning "the land of flowers") due to its lush, verdant landscape and because he arrived during the Easter season, which is known as "Pascua Florida" in Spanish.

Ponce de León's initial landing marked the beginning of Spanish interest in Florida, but it was not until later expeditions that more serious attempts at colonization were made. One such expedition was led by Pánfilo de Narváez in 1528. Narváez's mission, however, ended in disaster. After landing near Tampa Bay, his expedition faced numerous challenges, including hostile encounters with Indigenous peoples, treacherous swamps, and a lack of supplies. Narváez and his men ultimately failed to establish a permanent settlement, and only a handful of survivors, including Álvar Núñez Cabeza de Vaca, managed to make their way to Mexico after years of wandering.

Despite these early setbacks, the Spanish Crown remained determined to establish a foothold in Florida. This determination was partly fueled by strategic considerations. Florida's geographical position made it a key area for controlling the Gulf of Mexico and protecting Spanish shipping routes from the Caribbean to Europe. It was also seen as a potential buffer against French and English encroachments in the region.

One of the most significant Spanish attempts to colonize Florida occurred in 1539 when Hernando de Soto, a seasoned explorer and conquistador, led a large expedition into the region. De Soto's expedition was ambitious and well-funded, consisting of around 600 men, including soldiers, priests, craftsmen, and slaves. De Soto's goal was to explore and conquer the interior of the southeastern United States, searching for riches and potential sites for settlement. Over the course of four years, De Soto's expedition traveled through present-day Florida, Georgia, the Carolinas, Tennessee, Alabama, Mississippi, and Arkansas. They encountered numerous Indigenous communities, some of which were hostile, and De Soto's men were often engaged in violent conflicts. De Soto himself died in 1542 on the banks of the Mississippi River, and the remnants of his expedition eventually made their way to Mexico.

The Spanish Crown's continued interest in Florida led to further expeditions and efforts to establish permanent settlements. In 1559, Tristán de Luna y Arellano attempted to create a colony at Pensacola Bay. However, this venture also ended in failure due to hurricanes, supply shortages, and conflicts with Indigenous peoples. It wasn't until 1565 that the Spanish successfully established a lasting presence in Florida with the founding of St. Augustine by Pedro Menéndez de Avilés. St. Augustine is the oldest continuously occupied European-established settlement in the continental United States.

Menéndez was appointed as the governor of Florida and tasked with driving out the French, who had established a fort at Fort Caroline near present-day Jacksonville.

The rivalry between the Spanish and the French in Florida reached a climax in 1565 when Menéndez launched an attack on Fort Caroline, capturing it and killing most of the French inhabitants. This decisive action secured Spanish control over Florida and eliminated French competition in the region. Menéndez then focused on building and fortifying St. Augustine, which became the administrative and military center of Spanish Florida.

The establishment of St. Augustine marked the beginning of a more stable period of Spanish colonization in Florida. The Spanish implemented a system of missions, where Franciscan friars worked to convert Indigenous peoples to Christianity and integrate them into Spanish colonial society. The mission system extended throughout northern Florida and into present-day Georgia. These missions served both religious and economic purposes, facilitating the spread of Christianity and Spanish culture while also helping to secure Spanish territorial claims.

The relationship between the Spanish colonizers and the Indigenous peoples of Florida was complex and often fraught with tension. While some Indigenous groups allied with the Spanish and converted to Christianity, others resisted Spanish encroachment on their lands and sovereignty. The Spanish introduced new crops, livestock, and technologies to the region, which had both positive and negative impacts on Indigenous societies. Diseases brought by the Europeans also had devastating effects on the native populations, leading to significant demographic declines.

Throughout the 17th and 18th centuries, Spanish Florida faced numerous challenges. The colony was frequently threatened by rival European powers, particularly the British, who established colonies to the north in the Carolinas and Georgia. The Spanish and British engaged in a series of conflicts, including the War of Jenkins' Ear (1739-1748) and the Seven Years' War (1756-1763), which had significant repercussions for Florida. In 1763, as part of the Treaty of Paris, which ended the Seven Years' War, Spain ceded Florida to Britain in exchange for Havana, Cuba, which the British had captured during the war. This marked the beginning of British rule in Florida, which lasted until 1783.

During the period of British rule, Florida was divided into East Florida, with its capital at St. Augustine, and West Florida, with its capital at Pensacola. The British encouraged settlement and development in the region, attracting settlers from the American colonies and introducing new agricultural practices. However, the British period was relatively short-lived. In 1783, following the American Revolutionary War, the Treaty of Paris returned Florida to Spanish control as part of the broader geopolitical settlements of the time.

The second Spanish period in Florida, from 1783 to 1821, was marked by significant changes and challenges. The Spanish faced increasing pressure from American settlers moving into the region, as well as from Indigenous groups such as the Seminoles, who resisted Spanish authority and American encroachment. The Spanish struggled to maintain control over Florida, and the region became a refuge for runaway slaves and a base for pirate activities.

In 1819, the Adams-Onís Treaty was signed between Spain and the United States, ceding Florida to the United States in exchange for the American government's assumption of Spanish debts and the renunciation of claims to Texas. The transfer of Florida to the United States was formalized in 1821, marking the end of Spanish rule in the region.

The legacy of Spanish colonization in Florida is multifaceted and enduring. Spanish influence is evident in the region's architecture, place names, and cultural practices. St. Augustine, with its historic buildings and fortifications, stands as a testament to the Spanish colonial era. The interactions between the Spanish and Indigenous peoples left a lasting impact on the cultural and demographic landscape of Florida. The mission system, while often coercive and disruptive, also facilitated cultural exchanges and the blending of Spanish and Indigenous traditions.

The Spanish period in Florida also set the stage for future conflicts and developments. The establishment of European settlements and the displacement of Indigenous peoples created patterns of land use and social organization that would continue to evolve under subsequent British and American rule. The strategic importance of Florida, recognized by the Spanish, continued to be a key factor in its history, influencing military and political decisions well into the 19th and 20th centuries.

Chapter 30: British Settlements in Canada

The story of British settlements in Canada is a sweeping saga that unfolds over several centuries, beginning in the late 16th century and continuing through the 19th century. It is a tale marked by exploration, colonization, conflict, and transformation. The British presence in Canada significantly influenced the social, economic, and political development of the region, leaving an indelible mark on its history.

The origins of British interest in Canada can be traced back to the era of exploration in the late 15th and early 16th centuries. Although the Italian explorer John Cabot, sailing under the English flag, reached the coast of what is now Newfoundland in 1497, it was not until the early 17th century that the British began to establish a more permanent presence in North America. The early British efforts at colonization were driven by a variety of motives, including the search for new trade routes, the desire for economic gain, and the ambition to expand the British Empire.

One of the earliest and most significant British settlements in Canada was the founding of Newfoundland. In 1583, Sir Humphrey Gilbert claimed Newfoundland for England, establishing the first British colony in North America. However, it was not until the early 17th century that more sustained efforts to colonize the region took place. The fishing grounds off the coast of Newfoundland were particularly attractive to British and European fishermen, and the settlement of St. John's became a key hub for the fishing industry. The seasonal migration of fishermen eventually led to more permanent settlements as the economic opportunities in the region became more apparent.

The establishment of the Hudson's Bay Company (HBC) in 1670 marked a pivotal moment in the history of British settlements in

Canada. The HBC was granted a royal charter by King Charles II, giving it exclusive trading rights in the vast Hudson Bay watershed, an area known as Rupert's Land. The company established trading posts and forts throughout the region, including Fort Albany, York Factory, and Moose Factory. These posts served as centers for the fur trade, where Indigenous trappers exchanged furs for European goods. The HBC's operations significantly expanded British influence in the interior of Canada and laid the groundwork for future settlements.

The British presence in Canada was further solidified through a series of conflicts and treaties with other European powers, particularly France. The struggle for control of North America between Britain and France culminated in the Seven Years' War (1756-1763), known in North America as the French and Indian War. The conflict saw significant military engagements, including the Battle of the Plains of Abraham in 1759, where British forces under General James Wolfe defeated the French troops led by the Marquis de Montcalm, leading to the capture of Quebec City. The Treaty of Paris, signed in 1763, officially ended the war and ceded control of New France (modern-day Quebec) to Britain, dramatically expanding British territory in North America.

With the acquisition of New France, the British faced the challenge of governing a predominantly French-speaking and Catholic population. The Quebec Act of 1774 was a crucial piece of legislation that sought to address these challenges. The Act allowed the French inhabitants to retain their language, religion, and legal system, while also extending the boundaries of Quebec to include the Ohio Valley. This policy of accommodation helped to mitigate potential unrest and laid the foundation for the coexistence of French and British cultures in Canada.

The American Revolutionary War (1775-1783) had a profound impact on British settlements in Canada. Following the war, thousands of Loyalists—American colonists who remained loyal to the British

Crown—fled to Canada to escape persecution and seek refuge. These Loyalists significantly increased the population of British North America and contributed to the development of new settlements, particularly in what are now the provinces of Ontario and New Brunswick. The influx of Loyalists also led to the creation of Upper Canada (modern-day Ontario) and Lower Canada (modern-day Quebec) in 1791, each with its own government and institutions, as part of the Constitutional Act of 1791.

Throughout the 19th century, British settlements in Canada continued to expand westward. The fur trade, initially dominated by the HBC, played a central role in this expansion. The merger of the HBC and its rival, the North West Company, in 1821 consolidated British control over the fur trade in the western territories. The establishment of trading posts and forts, such as Fort Vancouver and Fort Edmonton, facilitated further exploration and settlement in the vast interior regions.

The early 19th century also saw increased immigration from Britain and other parts of Europe. The Napoleonic Wars and economic hardships in Europe prompted many to seek new opportunities in British North America. The British government encouraged this migration, viewing it as a means to populate and develop the colonies. Settlers were drawn to areas such as Upper Canada, the Maritime provinces, and later, the prairie regions. This wave of immigration contributed to the growth of towns and agricultural communities, shaping the demographic and cultural landscape of Canada.

The mid-19th century was a period of significant political and social change in British North America. The Rebellions of 1837-1838, which took place in Upper and Lower Canada, were driven by demands for responsible government and political reform. Although the rebellions were ultimately unsuccessful, they highlighted the growing discontent with the colonial administration. In response, the British government appointed Lord Durham to investigate the causes of the unrest. His report, published in 1839, recommended the unification of Upper and Lower Canada and the introduction of responsible government. These recommendations led to the passage of the Act of Union in 1840, which created the Province of Canada, and paved the way for the eventual establishment of a more democratic system of governance.

The movement towards Confederation in the mid-19th century was driven by a combination of economic, political, and security concerns. The British North America Act of 1867, also known as the Constitution Act, united the provinces of Canada (Ontario and Quebec), New Brunswick, and Nova Scotia into the Dominion of Canada. This act marked the beginning of a new phase in Canadian history, as the country gained greater autonomy while remaining part of the British Empire. The Confederation was motivated by the desire to create a more unified and stable political entity, capable of addressing internal divisions and external threats.

The expansion of the Canadian Confederation continued in the latter half of the 19th century and into the early 20th century. The acquisition of Rupert's Land and the North-Western Territory from the HBC in 1870, followed by the creation of the provinces of Manitoba, British Columbia, Saskatchewan, and Alberta, extended Canadian territory from the Atlantic to the Pacific. The construction of the Canadian Pacific Railway, completed in 1885, was a monumental engineering feat that connected the eastern and western parts of the country, facilitating the movement of people and goods, and fostering economic development.

The British settlements in Canada were also shaped by interactions with Indigenous peoples. The fur trade and the establishment of trading posts brought Europeans into contact with Indigenous communities, leading to complex relationships characterized by both cooperation and conflict. Treaties were negotiated between the British Crown and Indigenous nations, often with the aim of securing land for settlement and resource exploitation. These treaties, however, were frequently marked by misunderstandings and unequal power dynamics, leading to long-term consequences for Indigenous peoples. The imposition of European laws, cultural assimilation policies, and the establishment of residential schools had devastating effects on Indigenous communities, a legacy that continues to impact Canada today.

British settlements in Canada also played a significant role in the broader context of the British Empire. Canada became an important part of the imperial trade network, exporting raw materials such as timber, furs, and fish to Britain, while importing manufactured goods. The strategic location of Canada, with its vast natural resources and access to both the Atlantic and Pacific oceans, made it a valuable asset for the British Empire. Canadian ports and naval bases were integral to British military and economic interests, particularly during periods of conflict such as the War of 1812 and the two World Wars.

The cultural and social influence of British settlers in Canada is evident in many aspects of Canadian society. English became the dominant language, and British legal, political, and educational systems were established. British cultural practices, traditions, and institutions were transplanted to Canada, shaping the country's identity. However, this British influence coexisted with French, Indigenous, and other cultural elements, creating a unique and diverse Canadian mosaic.

The legacy of British settlements in Canada is complex and multifaceted. On one hand, British colonization brought significant economic development, political institutions, and cultural influences that have shaped modern Canada. On the other hand, it also involved the displacement and marginalization of Indigenous peoples, whose lands were appropriated, and whose cultures were suppressed. The history of British settlements in Canada is a story of exploration and expansion, but also of conflict and coexistence, reflecting the broader dynamics of colonialism and its lasting impacts.

151

Chapter 31: French Colonization of Louisiana

The French colonization of Louisiana is a fascinating and intricate chapter in the history of North America, spanning from the late 17th century until the early 19th century. This period saw the establishment of a French colonial presence in a vast and diverse region, which today encompasses parts of the modern United States, including the states of Louisiana, Arkansas, Missouri, Iowa, Oklahoma, Kansas, Nebraska, and parts of Minnesota, North Dakota, and South Dakota. The story of French Louisiana is characterized by exploration, settlement, economic development, cultural exchange, and conflict.

The French interest in the Mississippi Valley began in the late 17th century, motivated by both strategic and economic factors. The French were eager to expand their influence in North America and to counter the growing presence of the British and Spanish. Additionally, they sought to exploit the region's natural resources and to establish profitable trade networks. The French exploration of Louisiana can be traced back to the expeditions of Louis Jolliet and Father Jacques Marquette, who explored the Mississippi River in 1673, and René-Robert Cavelier, Sieur de La Salle, who followed the river to its mouth in 1682. La Salle claimed the entire Mississippi Valley for France, naming it Louisiana in honor of King Louis XIV.

La Salle's ambitious plans to establish a colony at the mouth of the Mississippi River initially ended in failure. In 1684, he launched an expedition to create a settlement near the Gulf of Mexico, but his fleet missed the mouth of the Mississippi and landed instead on the coast of Texas. The colony, beset by misfortune and conflict, ultimately collapsed, and La Salle was killed by his own men. Despite this setback, the French Crown remained committed to establishing a presence in Louisiana.

In 1699, Pierre Le Moyne d'Iberville, a seasoned French naval officer, led a successful expedition to the Gulf Coast. Iberville established the first permanent French settlement in the region at Biloxi Bay, in present-day Mississippi. This settlement served as a base for further exploration and colonization. Iberville's younger brother, Jean-Baptiste Le Moyne de Bienville, played a crucial role in the development of French Louisiana. Bienville founded the city of New Orleans in 1718, strategically located near the mouth of the Mississippi River. New Orleans quickly became the administrative and commercial center of the colony.

The French colonization of Louisiana was characterized by a mix of military, economic, and cultural endeavors. The French sought to create a profitable colony by exploiting the region's natural resources, including furs, timber, and agricultural products. The fur trade, in particular, was a major economic activity, with French traders establishing networks with Indigenous peoples throughout the Mississippi Valley. The French also introduced cash crops such as indigo, tobacco, and sugarcane, which were cultivated on plantations using enslaved African labor.

The French colonial administration in Louisiana faced numerous challenges, including conflicts with Indigenous peoples, rival European powers, and internal governance issues. Relations with Indigenous communities were complex and varied. The French formed alliances with some tribes, such as the Choctaw and the Illinois Confederation, while they clashed with others, including the Natchez and the Chickasaw. These alliances and conflicts had significant impacts on the dynamics of power and trade in the region.

The French efforts to colonize Louisiana were also marked by competition with other European powers. The Spanish controlled Florida and the Gulf Coast to the east and west of Louisiana, while the British were expanding their colonies along the Atlantic seaboard and into the Ohio Valley. The geopolitical rivalry between France, Britain, and Spain often played out in Louisiana, with the colony serving as a frontier of imperial conflict.

One of the most significant conflicts during the French colonial period was the Natchez Rebellion of 1729-1731. The Natchez, an Indigenous group living near the Mississippi River, launched a coordinated attack on the French settlers in retaliation for encroachments on their land and other grievances. The rebellion resulted in the deaths of hundreds of French colonists and the near destruction of the Natchez community. The French response was brutal, with military campaigns aimed at crushing the rebellion and punishing the Natchez. This conflict highlighted the volatile nature of colonial-Indigenous relations in Louisiana.

The economic development of French Louisiana was hindered by a range of factors, including the colony's remote location, a lack of investment, and a challenging environment. The early settlers faced difficulties in establishing sustainable agricultural practices due to the region's swamps, floods, and diseases. Additionally, the colony struggled with a shortage of labor and resources. To address these challenges, the French government and private investors implemented various schemes to attract settlers and laborers to Louisiana. These efforts included offering land grants, recruiting immigrants from Europe, and importing enslaved Africans to work on plantations.

The introduction of enslaved Africans to Louisiana had profound and lasting impacts on the colony's social and economic structure. Enslaved people were brought to Louisiana primarily to work on indigo, tobacco, and sugarcane plantations. The brutal system of chattel slavery became a central component of the colony's economy, with enslaved Africans playing a crucial role in its development. The Code Noir, a set of regulations governing the treatment of enslaved people in French colonies, was implemented in Louisiana in 1724. While it ostensibly provided some protections for enslaved people, in practice it reinforced their subjugation and exploitation.

The demographic composition of French Louisiana was diverse and multicultural. In addition to French settlers and enslaved Africans, the colony was home to Indigenous peoples and immigrants from other parts of Europe, including Germans, Spaniards, and Acadians (French-speaking settlers from present-day Canada). This diversity contributed to a unique cultural milieu in Louisiana, characterized by a blending of French, African, Indigenous, and other influences. The Creole culture that emerged in Louisiana was a product of this cultural fusion, with distinctive traditions, cuisine, music, and language.

The French colonial period in Louisiana came to an end in the mid-18th century as a result of geopolitical shifts and conflicts in Europe and North America. The Seven Years' War (1756-1763), known in North America as the French and Indian War, was a global conflict that pitted France against Britain and their respective allies. The war had significant repercussions for French colonial holdings in North America. The Treaty of Paris, signed in 1763, marked the conclusion of the war and resulted in major territorial changes. France ceded Canada and its territories east of the Mississippi River to Britain, while Spain, which had allied with France during the war, received Louisiana west of the Mississippi, including New Orleans.

The transfer of Louisiana to Spanish control marked the beginning of a new chapter in the region's history. The Spanish period (1763-1803) saw a continuation of many aspects of French colonial society, including the use of French language and customs, but also brought about significant administrative and economic changes. Spanish authorities implemented reforms aimed at improving the colony's governance and economic productivity. They encouraged immigration, invested in infrastructure, and sought to strengthen the defense of the colony against potential threats.

Despite these efforts, Spanish rule in Louisiana faced challenges, including resistance from the French-speaking population and ongoing conflicts with Indigenous peoples. Additionally, the geopolitical landscape of North America continued to evolve, with the American Revolution (1775-1783) leading to the establishment of the United States and changing the balance of power in the region.

The final chapter of French influence in Louisiana came with the Louisiana Purchase of 1803. In a surprising turn of events, France briefly regained control of Louisiana in 1800 through the Treaty of San Ildefonso, in which Spain secretly ceded the territory back to France. However, French control was short-lived. Facing financial difficulties and the threat of conflict with Britain, Napoleon Bonaparte decided to sell Louisiana to the United States. The Louisiana Purchase, finalized in 1803, doubled the size of the United States and opened up vast new territories for exploration and settlement.

The legacy of French colonization in Louisiana is profound and enduring. The French established the foundations of the region's economic, social, and cultural structures. The city of New Orleans, with its distinctive French Quarter, remains a testament to the French colonial era. The Creole culture that emerged in Louisiana, characterized by a unique blend of French, African, Indigenous, and other influences, continues to thrive and shape the region's identity. French legal traditions, such as the use of civil law, also persist in Louisiana, distinguishing it from other states in the United States.

Chapter 32: Dutch Rule in Suriname

The history of Dutch rule in Suriname is a rich and complex narrative that spans from the early 17th century to the country's independence in the 20th century. This period is marked by colonization, economic exploitation, the establishment of a plantation economy, interactions with Indigenous peoples and enslaved Africans, and eventual movements towards emancipation and independence. The Dutch influence left an indelible mark on Suriname's social, economic, and cultural landscape, shaping the nation in profound ways.

The Dutch interest in Suriname began in the early 17th century as part of their broader ambitions in the Caribbean and South America. The Dutch West India Company (WIC) was established in 1621 with the goal of challenging Spanish and Portuguese dominance in the Atlantic. The WIC sought to establish profitable colonies and trading posts, and Suriname, with its fertile land and strategic location, was an attractive prospect. In 1650, an English settler named Lord Willoughby of Parham established the first European settlement in Suriname, but the Dutch quickly moved to assert their control.

In 1667, during the Second Anglo-Dutch War, the Dutch captured Suriname from the English. The Treaty of Breda, which ended the war, formalized Dutch control over the territory. The Dutch named the colony "Dutch Guiana" and began to develop it as a plantation economy. The fertile soil and favorable climate of Suriname made it ideal for growing sugar, coffee, cacao, and other cash crops. The establishment of a plantation economy required a large labor force, and the Dutch turned to the transatlantic slave trade to meet this need.

The importation of enslaved Africans was central to the economic development of Dutch Suriname. The WIC and private planters brought tens of thousands of enslaved Africans to work on the plantations. These individuals were subjected to brutal conditions, forced to toil under the harsh tropical sun, and endure physical punishment and exploitation. The system of chattel slavery in Suriname was characterized by extreme cruelty and dehumanization. Enslaved Africans were treated as property, denied basic human rights, and subjected to severe punishments for any form of resistance.

Despite these harsh conditions, enslaved Africans in Suriname demonstrated remarkable resilience and resistance. One of the most notable forms of resistance was marronage, the act of escaping from plantations to establish independent communities in the interior of the country. These communities, known as Maroon societies, were formed by escaped slaves who sought freedom and autonomy in the dense rainforest. The Maroons developed their own distinct cultures, languages, and social structures, drawing on African traditions and adapting to their new environment. They engaged in guerrilla warfare against the Dutch, conducting raids on plantations and freeing other enslaved people.

The Surinamese Maroons played a significant role in the history of Dutch rule in Suriname. The most famous Maroon leader was Boni, who led a successful resistance movement in the 18th century. The Dutch were unable to fully subdue the Maroons and eventually entered into treaties with them, recognizing their autonomy in certain regions in exchange for an end to hostilities. These treaties, however, were often fragile and frequently violated by both sides.

In addition to the Maroons, the Indigenous peoples of Suriname also played a crucial role in the colony's history. The Arawak, Carib, and other Indigenous groups inhabited the region long before European arrival. The Dutch established trade relations with some Indigenous communities, exchanging goods such as metal tools, weapons, and textiles for food, labor, and local knowledge. However, the expansion of Dutch plantations often led to conflicts over land and resources. The Dutch employed a variety of strategies to subjugate Indigenous peoples, including military force, alliances, and treaties.

The economic success of the plantation system in Suriname brought considerable wealth to the Dutch colonists, but it also reinforced a rigid and hierarchical social structure. The colony was characterized by stark divisions based on race and class. The white European planters and administrators occupied the top of the social hierarchy, enjoying significant wealth and power. Below them were the free people of color, who often included mixed-race individuals and freed slaves. At the bottom were the enslaved Africans, who endured the harshest conditions and had the fewest rights.

The abolitionist movement in the Netherlands gained momentum in the late 18th and early 19th centuries, leading to increasing pressure to end slavery in Suriname. The British abolition of the transatlantic slave trade in 1807 and the subsequent pressure on other European powers to follow suit further contributed to this shift. In 1814, the Dutch government officially abolished the transatlantic slave trade, although illegal smuggling of enslaved people continued for several years.

The formal abolition of slavery in Suriname did not occur until July 1, 1863. This date, known as Emancipation Day, marked the end of legal slavery in the Dutch colonies. However, the transition from slavery to freedom was not immediate. The Dutch implemented a system of "apprenticeship" that required freed slaves to continue working on the plantations for a period of ten years under conditions that closely resembled slavery. It was only in 1873 that full emancipation was granted, and the formerly enslaved people were free to leave the plantations and seek other forms of employment.

The abolition of slavery had profound effects on the social and economic structure of Suriname. The plantation economy faced significant challenges as the labor force transitioned from coerced to free labor. To address labor shortages, the Dutch brought in indentured laborers from other parts of the world, including India, Java (Indonesia), and China. These laborers signed contracts to work for a fixed period, usually five years, in exchange for passage to Suriname, wages, and the promise of a return trip or land grants. The introduction of indentured labor added new layers of complexity to Suriname's demographic and cultural landscape.

The late 19th and early 20th centuries saw significant social, economic, and political changes in Suriname. The decline of the plantation economy led to diversification in agriculture and the rise of new economic activities, such as mining and forestry. Urbanization increased, particularly in the capital city of Paramaribo, which became a melting pot of cultures and ethnicities. The political landscape also began to change, with growing demands for greater local autonomy and representation.

The struggle for political independence in Suriname gained momentum in the mid-20th century. In 1948, the Netherlands granted Suriname internal self-government, allowing for greater local control over domestic affairs. This period saw the rise of political parties and movements advocating for full independence. The nationalist movement in Suriname was influenced by broader decolonization trends in the Caribbean and around the world.

On November 25, 1975, Suriname achieved full independence from the Netherlands. The transition to independence was marked by both optimism and challenges. The new nation faced the task of building a cohesive national identity from its diverse cultural and ethnic groups. The legacy of colonialism, including economic dependency and social inequalities, continued to shape Suriname's development.

The Dutch colonial legacy in Suriname is evident in many aspects of the nation's culture, language, and institutions. Dutch remains an official language and is widely used in government, education, and media. The legal system in Suriname is based on Dutch civil law, and many cultural practices, such as architecture, cuisine, and festivals, reflect Dutch influences.

At the same time, Suriname's rich multicultural heritage is a testament to the diverse contributions of its Indigenous peoples, Africans, Asians, and Europeans. The blending of these cultures has created a unique and vibrant society. Traditional Maroon communities continue to thrive, preserving their distinct languages, customs, and way of life. The descendants of indentured laborers from India, Indonesia, and China have also maintained their cultural identities while contributing to the broader national culture.

In recent decades, Suriname has faced various challenges, including political instability, economic difficulties, and social inequalities. The legacy of Dutch rule and the impacts of globalization continue to influence the nation's development. However, Suriname has also made strides in building a democratic society, promoting cultural diversity, and fostering economic growth.

Chapter 33: Portuguese Control of Macau

The Portuguese control of Macau is a fascinating and intricate chapter in the history of colonialism, marked by complex interactions between European and Asian powers, cultural exchanges, economic developments, and the gradual evolution of political control. The story of Macau under Portuguese rule spans over four centuries, from the 16th century until its handover to China in 1999. Throughout this period, Macau served as a crucial gateway for trade between Europe and Asia, a melting pot of cultures, and a site of significant historical events.

The origins of Portuguese presence in Macau date back to the early 16th century, a time when Portugal was establishing itself as a dominant maritime power. Following the successful expeditions to India by Vasco da Gama and the establishment of a colonial base in Goa, the Portuguese were eager to expand their influence further east. The lucrative trade with China and Japan, especially in silk, porcelain, and spices, made the region highly attractive.

The Portuguese first arrived on the southern coast of China in the early 1510s. They sought to establish a foothold in the region to facilitate their trade ambitions. In 1513, the Portuguese explorer Jorge Álvares reached the Pearl River Delta, marking the beginning of direct contact between Portugal and China. Initial encounters were often tense, characterized by both trade and conflict. The Portuguese engaged in trade with local Chinese merchants but also clashed with Chinese authorities due to their aggressive tactics and attempts to establish fortified positions.

The establishment of a permanent Portuguese settlement in Macau occurred around 1557. According to historical records, the Portuguese were allowed to settle in Macau in exchange for helping the Ming dynasty authorities suppress coastal piracy, which had been a significant problem in the region. The precise terms of the agreement between the Portuguese and the Chinese authorities remain a subject of historical debate. Some sources suggest that the Portuguese paid an annual rent to the Chinese government, while others argue that the arrangement was more informal, based on mutual benefit rather than a formal lease.

Once established in Macau, the Portuguese quickly developed the settlement into a thriving trading post. Macau's strategic location at the mouth of the Pearl River Delta made it an ideal hub for trade between China, Japan, Southeast Asia, and Europe. The Portuguese capitalized on the lucrative trade in silk, porcelain, spices, and other luxury goods. Macau became a key link in the transcontinental trade network, connecting the markets of Europe with those of East Asia.

The Portuguese administration in Macau was relatively autonomous, although nominally under the jurisdiction of the Portuguese Viceroy in Goa. The local governance was primarily in the hands of the Senado da Câmara, a municipal council composed of prominent Portuguese settlers and merchants. This body was responsible for the administration of the colony, including matters of trade, law, and order. The Portuguese authorities also established fortifications and a military presence to defend the settlement against potential threats, including pirate attacks and rival colonial powers.

One of the most significant aspects of Portuguese rule in Macau was the cultural and religious influence they brought to the region. The Portuguese introduced Roman Catholicism to Macau, and the city became an important center for missionary activity in East Asia. The Jesuits, in particular, played a crucial role in the cultural exchange between Europe and China. Notable Jesuit missionaries such as Matteo Ricci and Francis Xavier used Macau as a base for their missions into mainland China and Japan. They sought to convert local populations to Christianity, but their efforts also facilitated the exchange of knowledge and ideas between East and West.

The architectural and cultural landscape of Macau during the Portuguese period reflected this blend of influences. Churches, such as the iconic St. Paul's Cathedral, were built alongside traditional Chinese temples. The city's layout, with its narrow streets and colonial-style buildings, showcased a fusion of Portuguese and Chinese architectural styles. The Portuguese also introduced Western education, legal systems, and other aspects of European culture to Macau, creating a unique cultural hybrid that still defines the city's character today.

The economic prosperity of Macau during the early period of Portuguese rule was not without its challenges. The Portuguese faced competition from other European powers, such as the Dutch and the Spanish, who sought to establish their own footholds in the region. The Dutch, in particular, posed a significant threat to Portuguese dominance in the 17th century. They launched several attacks on Macau, the most notable being the Battle of Macau in 1622. Despite being heavily outnumbered, the Portuguese defenders, with the help of local Chinese and African residents, successfully repelled the Dutch assault, securing Macau's status as a Portuguese stronghold.

The relationship between the Portuguese and the Chinese authorities in Macau was complex and often fraught with tension. While the Portuguese enjoyed a significant degree of autonomy within the colony, they were always aware of their status as foreign settlers in Chinese territory. The Chinese authorities maintained a watchful eye over Macau, imposing various restrictions and regulations to ensure that Portuguese activities did not undermine Chinese sovereignty. For example, the Chinese restricted the construction of defensive walls around Macau, reflecting their concern over the potential for the settlement to become a fortified enclave.

In the 18th and 19th centuries, the fortunes of Macau began to wane. The rise of other colonial powers in the region, along with the opening of new trade routes, diminished Macau's role as a primary trading hub. The British establishment of Hong Kong in 1842, following the First Opium War, was a significant blow to Macau's economic status. Hong Kong's deep-water harbor and favorable trade conditions quickly attracted merchants and traders, drawing commerce away from Macau.

The decline in trade was accompanied by social and political changes. The Portuguese authorities faced growing challenges in maintaining control over the colony. Internal conflicts, economic difficulties, and pressure from both local Chinese residents and foreign powers complicated the administration of Macau. The Opium Wars and the subsequent treaties imposed by Western powers on China further destabilized the region, affecting Macau's position within the broader geopolitical landscape.

Despite these challenges, Macau remained under Portuguese control throughout the 19th and early 20th centuries. The Portuguese government made efforts to modernize the colony, introducing infrastructure improvements, public services, and administrative reforms. However, these efforts were often limited by financial constraints and the complex political dynamics of the region.

The 20th century brought significant changes to Macau's political status. The Chinese Revolution of 1911, which led to the fall of the Qing dynasty and the establishment of the Republic of China, had a profound impact on Macau. The new Chinese government asserted its sovereignty over all former Qing territories, including Macau. While the Portuguese continued to administer the colony, their position was increasingly precarious in the face of growing Chinese nationalism and demands for the return of Chinese territories under foreign control.

The Second World War and the subsequent Chinese Civil War further complicated the situation in Macau. The Japanese occupation of nearby regions, including Hong Kong, during World War II, isolated Macau and created economic hardships. However, Macau itself was not occupied by Japanese forces, allowing it to serve as a neutral haven for refugees and a base for clandestine activities.

In the post-war period, the rise of the People's Republic of China (PRC) under the leadership of the Communist Party brought new challenges to Portuguese control of Macau. The PRC, established in 1949, asserted its claim over all Chinese territories, including Macau. The Portuguese government, facing internal and external pressures, entered into negotiations with the PRC to address the status of Macau. In 1974, the Carnation Revolution in Portugal led to a shift in Portuguese colonial policy, with the new government seeking to decolonize its overseas territories.

Formal negotiations between Portugal and China regarding the future of Macau began in the 1980s. These discussions culminated in the Sino-Portuguese Joint Declaration of 1987, which outlined the terms for the transfer of sovereignty over Macau from Portugal to China. According to the agreement, Macau would become a Special Administrative Region (SAR) of China, with a high degree of autonomy for 50 years after the handover. The "one country, two systems" principle, which had also been applied to Hong Kong, was designed to ensure the preservation of Macau's unique social, economic, and legal systems.

The official handover of Macau to China took place on December 20, 1999, marking the end of over 400 years of Portuguese rule. The event was a significant milestone in the history of both Portugal and China, symbolizing the resolution of a complex colonial legacy and the beginning of a new era for Macau. The transition was relatively smooth, with the local population and international community closely observing the implementation of the "one country, two systems" framework.

Since the handover, Macau has undergone significant transformations. The region has experienced rapid economic growth, driven primarily by the gaming and tourism industries. Macau has become one of the world's leading gambling destinations, attracting millions of visitors annually. The local government has invested in infrastructure, education, and public services, contributing to improved living standards for residents.

Culturally, Macau continues to reflect its unique blend of Portuguese and Chinese influences. The historic center of Macau, with its colonial-era architecture, has been designated a UNESCO World Heritage Site, recognizing its historical and cultural significance. Festivals, cuisine, and traditions from both Portuguese and Chinese cultures are celebrated, contributing to Macau's vibrant cultural landscape.

Chapter 34: British Influence in Hong Kong

The British influence in Hong Kong is a profound and intricate narrative that spans over a century and a half, marked by dramatic transformations, socio-economic developments, and a unique fusion of Eastern and Western cultures. This history begins in the early 19th century and extends until the handover of Hong Kong to China in 1997. The British colonial period in Hong Kong is characterized by its role as a strategic trading post, a hub of international commerce, and a site of significant political and social change.

The origins of British interest in Hong Kong can be traced back to the early 19th century during the height of the British Empire's expansion and the increasing importance of trade with China. At that time, the British were deeply engaged in the trade of goods such as tea, silk, and porcelain from China. However, the trade was heavily imbalanced, as China had little interest in British products, leading to a significant outflow of silver from Britain. To address this trade deficit, the British began exporting opium, produced in British India, to China. The widespread addiction to opium in China led to significant social and economic problems, prompting the Qing dynasty to take measures to curtail the opium trade.

Tensions over the opium trade culminated in the First Opium War (1839-1842) between Britain and China. The conflict began after Chinese authorities seized and destroyed a large quantity of opium stored by British merchants in Canton (Guangzhou). In response, the British government dispatched a military expedition to China, leading to a series of battles along the Chinese coast. The superior military technology and naval power of the British forces resulted in a decisive victory over the Chinese.

The Treaty of Nanking, signed in 1842, formally ended the First Opium War and marked a significant turning point in Sino-British relations. Under the terms of the treaty, China ceded the island of Hong Kong to Britain "in perpetuity." The treaty also included provisions for the opening of five Chinese ports to British trade and residence, the establishment of a fixed tariff, and the granting of extraterritorial rights to British subjects in China. The acquisition of Hong Kong provided the British with a strategically located deep-water harbor that would become a vital base for their commercial and military activities in East Asia.

The early years of British rule in Hong Kong were focused on establishing the infrastructure and governance necessary to support the colony's development. The island was sparsely populated at the time of the British arrival, with a small fishing community and a few scattered villages. The British colonial administration, led by the first Governor of Hong Kong, Sir Henry Pottinger, embarked on a program of urban development and modernization. They laid out plans for the construction of roads, buildings, and other essential infrastructure. The establishment of Victoria City, named after Queen Victoria, marked the beginning of Hong Kong's transformation into a major urban center.

Economic development was a primary objective of the British colonial administration. Hong Kong's natural deep-water harbor, combined with its strategic location on the trade routes between Europe, Asia, and the Americas, made it an ideal hub for international commerce. The British encouraged free trade policies, low taxation, and minimal regulatory interference, creating a business-friendly environment that attracted merchants, traders, and entrepreneurs from around the world. The port of Hong Kong quickly became one of the busiest and most important in Asia, serving as a key transshipment point for goods and facilitating the flow of trade between East and West.

The economic prosperity of Hong Kong was accompanied by significant demographic changes. The population of the colony grew rapidly as people from various parts of China and other regions migrated to Hong Kong in search of opportunities. The influx of Chinese immigrants, in particular, transformed the social and cultural landscape of the colony. The British administration implemented policies to accommodate the diverse population, including the establishment of separate residential and commercial areas for different ethnic groups. The creation of a multicultural society, where Western and Chinese customs coexisted, became a defining feature of Hong Kong.

The Second Opium War (1856-1860), also known as the Arrow War, further expanded British control over Hong Kong. The conflict arose from ongoing disputes over trade rights, diplomatic relations, and the treatment of British subjects in China. The war ended with the signing of the Treaty of Tientsin in 1858 and the Convention of Peking in 1860. These agreements resulted in additional territorial concessions to Britain, including the Kowloon Peninsula and Stonecutters Island, which were ceded to the British. The acquisition of these areas provided more land for development and contributed to the growth of Hong Kong as a commercial and administrative center.

Throughout the late 19th and early 20th centuries, Hong Kong continued to thrive as a colonial outpost and international trading hub. The British administration invested in infrastructure projects, such as the construction of the Peak Tram, the establishment of the University of Hong Kong, and the development of public services and utilities. The colony's legal and educational systems were based on British models, which helped to establish a framework for governance and social order.

The social and cultural landscape of Hong Kong during this period reflected a blend of British and Chinese influences. British colonial officials, businessmen, and expatriates brought with them Western customs, traditions, and institutions. At the same time, the Chinese population maintained their cultural heritage, practices, and social structures. This coexistence of cultures led to the development of a unique hybrid identity that became a hallmark of Hong Kong society.

The Japanese occupation of Hong Kong during World War II (1941-1945) was a dark and tumultuous period in the colony's history. Following the attack on Pearl Harbor, Japanese forces launched an invasion of Hong Kong in December 1941. The British defenders, outnumbered and outgunned, surrendered after 18 days of fierce fighting. The Japanese occupation brought severe hardship to the people of Hong Kong, including widespread suffering, shortages of food and supplies, and harsh treatment by the occupying forces. The occupation ended with the Japanese surrender in August 1945, and British control was restored shortly thereafter.

The post-war period marked a new phase in Hong Kong's development. The colony experienced a dramatic economic transformation, driven by industrialization, trade, and investment. The influx of refugees from mainland China, fleeing the civil war and the establishment of the People's Republic of China (PRC) in 1949, contributed to the rapid growth of the population and labor force. Hong Kong's economy diversified, with the expansion of manufacturing, textiles, electronics, and financial services. The colony emerged as one of the "Four Asian Tigers," alongside South Korea, Taiwan, and Singapore, known for their rapid industrialization and economic growth.

The British colonial administration implemented policies to support economic development and improve living standards. Investments in infrastructure, housing, education, and healthcare were prioritized to accommodate the growing population and sustain economic growth. The construction of public housing estates, the expansion of transportation networks, and the establishment of new towns and industrial zones were key initiatives during this period.

Hong Kong's legal and political systems evolved as well. The British administration introduced reforms to enhance governance and public administration. The establishment of the Legislative Council (LegCo) provided a platform for representation and debate on public policies. However, the colonial government retained significant control over decision-making processes, and full democratic representation remained limited.

The approach of the end of British colonial rule in Hong Kong was shaped by geopolitical developments and negotiations between Britain and China. The signing of the Joint Declaration on the Question of Hong Kong in 1984 by British Prime Minister Margaret Thatcher and Chinese Premier Zhao Ziyang was a landmark agreement that outlined the terms for the transfer of sovereignty over Hong Kong from Britain to China. The declaration stipulated that Hong Kong would become a Special Administrative Region (SAR) of China, operating under the "one country, two systems" principle. This framework was designed to preserve Hong Kong's capitalist economy, legal system, and way of life for 50 years after the handover in 1997.

The final years of British rule were marked by preparations for the transition to Chinese sovereignty. The British administration undertook efforts to strengthen Hong Kong's institutions, promote democratic reforms, and ensure a smooth handover. The last Governor of Hong Kong, Chris Patten, introduced measures to expand the franchise and increase the representation of elected officials in the LegCo. These reforms aimed to enhance public participation and accountability in governance.

On July 1, 1997, the transfer of sovereignty over Hong Kong from Britain to China took place in a historic ceremony attended by dignitaries from both nations. The event marked the end of 156 years of British colonial rule and the beginning of a new era for Hong Kong under Chinese sovereignty. The handover was accompanied by a sense of optimism, uncertainty, and hope for the future.

Since the handover, Hong Kong has operated under the framework of "one country, two systems," which grants it a high degree of autonomy in most matters except foreign affairs and defense. The region has retained its legal system, capitalist economy, and social freedoms, distinguishing it from the mainland. Hong Kong continues to serve as a global financial center, a hub for trade and investment, and a cultural bridge between East and West.

However, the post-handover period has also been marked by significant challenges and tensions. Issues related to political representation, civil liberties, and the relationship between Hong Kong and the central government in Beijing have been sources of contention. The pro-democracy movement in Hong Kong has sought to advocate for greater political freedoms and democratic reforms, leading to mass protests and demonstrations at various points.

The most notable recent events include the 2014 Umbrella Movement, which called for universal suffrage and democratic elections, and the 2019-2020 anti-extradition bill protests, which evolved into broader demands for political reform and resistance to perceived encroachments on Hong Kong's autonomy. The implementation of the National Security Law in 2020 by the Chinese government has further intensified debates over the balance between maintaining Hong Kong's autonomy and ensuring national security.

Chapter 35: French Colonization of Quebec

The French colonization of Quebec, part of the larger French colonial empire in North America known as New France, began in the early 17th century and had profound and lasting impacts on the region's cultural, social, and political development. The primary motivations for French exploration and colonization were the pursuit of wealth through the fur trade, the desire to spread Christianity among Indigenous populations, and the geopolitical aim of expanding French influence in the face of competition from other European powers.

Samuel de Champlain, often referred to as the "Father of New France," played a pivotal role in establishing the French presence in Quebec. In 1608, Champlain founded the settlement of Quebec City, which became the administrative and cultural center of New France. Situated on the banks of the St. Lawrence River, the location was strategically chosen for its defensible position and its access to the interior of the continent, which was crucial for the fur trade. Champlain's leadership and diplomacy with Indigenous peoples, particularly the Huron-Wendat, were instrumental in ensuring the survival and growth of the colony. The alliances he forged allowed the French to access vital fur trade routes and secure military support against rival Indigenous groups and European competitors.

The fur trade quickly became the economic backbone of New France. French traders and coureurs des bois (independent traders) ventured deep into the interior, establishing a vast network of trade relationships with various Indigenous nations. The fur trade fostered a complex web of economic and social interactions, leading to the emergence of a distinct Métis culture, characterized by the blending of French and Indigenous customs, languages, and practices. The French reliance on Indigenous knowledge and cooperation underscored the interdependent nature of these relationships, which were often formalized through alliances and intermarriage.

The Jesuit missionaries, also known as the "Black Robes," were another significant element of French colonial efforts in Quebec. Their mission was to convert Indigenous peoples to Christianity, and they established missions throughout the region. The Jesuits documented their experiences in detailed accounts, providing valuable insights into Indigenous cultures and the challenges of missionary work. While their efforts met with varying degrees of success, the Jesuits were often seen as both spiritual leaders and intermediaries between the French and Indigenous communities. Their presence contributed to the cultural and religious landscape of New France and left a lasting legacy in the region.

French colonial society in Quebec was characterized by a hierarchical structure, with a small elite of landowners, known as seigneurs, at the top. The seigneurial system, modeled after the feudal system in France, involved granting large tracts of land to seigneurs, who then subdivided the land to habitant farmers in exchange for rents and dues. This system fostered agricultural development and a rural society based on small-scale farming. Habitants enjoyed a degree of independence and self-sufficiency, but they were also subject to the demands of the seigneurs and the Catholic Church, which played a central role in their daily lives.

The social fabric of Quebec was further shaped by the arrival of the filles du roi, or "King's Daughters," between 1663 and 1673. These young women were sent by the French crown to marry settlers and boost the population of New France. Their arrival helped stabilize the colony by creating family units and promoting demographic growth. The descendants of these early settlers became the foundation of Quebec's Francophone population, whose distinct cultural identity would endure despite subsequent British conquest and influence.

The geopolitical rivalry between France and Britain in North America culminated in a series of conflicts, most notably the Seven Years' War (1756-1763). The war's North American theater, known as the French and Indian War, saw the British and their Indigenous allies ultimately triumph over the French. The decisive Battle of the Plains of Abraham in 1759, where British forces under General James Wolfe defeated the French led by General Louis-Joseph de Montcalm, marked the fall of Quebec City and the beginning of the end for French rule in North America. The Treaty of Paris in 1763 formally ceded New France to Britain, reshaping the political landscape of the continent.

Despite the British conquest, the French-speaking population of Quebec retained much of its cultural and social distinctiveness. The British authorities, recognizing the impracticality of assimilating the Francophone population, enacted policies that allowed for the preservation of French civil law, the Catholic religion, and the seigneurial system. The Quebec Act of 1774 was a particularly significant piece of legislation that guaranteed these rights, ensuring the survival of French culture and language in the colony. This act also expanded the territory of Quebec to include the Great Lakes and Ohio Valley regions, which further entrenched French influence in North America.

The legacy of French colonization in Quebec is evident in the province's unique identity within Canada. The French language remains a dominant and official language, and Quebec's legal and educational systems are deeply rooted in French traditions. The province's cultural institutions, such as its literature, music, and cuisine, reflect a rich Francophone heritage that distinguishes it from the rest of Canada. The enduring presence of the Catholic Church, despite secularization trends, also underscores the lasting impact of French missionary efforts.

The relationship between Quebec and the rest of Canada has been marked by a complex interplay of cooperation, conflict, and accommodation. The Quiet Revolution of the 1960s, a period of intense social and political change, saw Quebec undergo rapid modernization and secularization, challenging the traditional dominance of the Church and seigneurial elites. This period also sparked a resurgence of Quebec nationalism, culminating in two referendums on sovereignty in 1980 and 1995. Although both referendums were ultimately unsuccessful, they highlighted the deep-seated desire for greater autonomy and recognition of Quebec's distinct identity within Canada.

In contemporary Quebec, the legacy of French colonization is celebrated and preserved through various cultural institutions, festivals, and educational programs. The province's rich history is a source of pride for many Quebecers, who view their Francophone heritage as a defining element of their identity. The preservation of the French language and culture remains a priority for the provincial government, which implements policies to promote and protect Francophone institutions and traditions.

The French colonization of Quebec was a complex and multifaceted process that left an indelible mark on the region. From the establishment of Quebec City by Samuel de Champlain to the thriving fur trade, the efforts of Jesuit missionaries, and the creation of a distinct Francophone society, the French colonial period laid the foundations for the unique cultural, social, and political identity of modern Quebec. Despite the challenges posed by British conquest and subsequent political changes, the legacy of French colonization endures, shaping the province's character and its place within the broader Canadian and North American contexts.

Chapter 36: Swedish Colonization of Delaware

The Swedish colonization of Delaware, known as New Sweden, was a relatively short but significant chapter in the colonial history of North America. This period, from 1638 to 1655, marked Sweden's attempt to establish itself as a colonial power in the New World, driven by ambitions of economic expansion and increased geopolitical influence. The Swedes, alongside a small number of Finns, settled along the Delaware River, laying the groundwork for future European settlements in the region and leaving a lasting cultural and historical legacy.

The backdrop to Swedish colonization efforts was the desire of the Swedish Empire, under the reign of King Gustavus Adolphus and later Queen Christina, to join the ranks of other European powers such as Spain, France, England, and the Netherlands, which were rapidly expanding their overseas empires. Sweden, a burgeoning power in Europe during the early 17th century, saw colonization as a means to bolster its economy through trade, particularly in fur and tobacco, and to create a strategic foothold in North America.

In 1637, the Swedish government, in collaboration with Dutch investors, organized an expedition to establish a colony in the New World. The venture was led by Peter Minuit, a former director of the Dutch colony of New Netherland, who had significant experience in colonial administration and negotiation with Indigenous peoples. Minuit set sail with two ships, the Kalmar Nyckel and the Fogel Grip, and arrived in the Delaware Bay in the spring of 1638. Upon arrival, Minuit negotiated with the local Lenape and Susquehannock tribes, securing land for the establishment of a settlement.

The first settlement, Fort Christina, named in honor of the young Queen Christina of Sweden, was established near present-day

Wilmington, Delaware. This fortification served as the administrative and military center of New Sweden. Fort Christina's location on the Christina River, a tributary of the Delaware River, was strategically chosen for its defensible position and access to the river, which was vital for trade and transportation. The early years of the colony were marked by efforts to build a sustainable community, cultivate crops, and establish trade relations with Indigenous tribes and nearby European colonies.

The population of New Sweden was a mix of Swedes, Finns, and a few Dutch and German settlers. The Finns, in particular, played a crucial role in the colony's development. They brought with them expertise in forestry and farming, including the practice of slash-and-burn agriculture, which was well-suited to the dense forests of the Delaware Valley. This agricultural technique involved clearing land by cutting and burning trees and then using the ash-enriched soil for farming. The Finns' contributions were vital in ensuring the colony's self-sufficiency and survival.

The Swedes engaged in the fur trade with the Indigenous populations, exchanging European goods such as metal tools, firearms, and textiles for valuable furs. This trade was the economic lifeblood of the colony and helped establish New Sweden as a viable enterprise. The Swedes also cultivated tobacco, which became a profitable cash crop. The economic activities of the colony, however, were modest compared to the larger and more established Dutch and English colonies in the region.

Despite its small size and limited resources, New Sweden managed to expand its territorial claims along the Delaware River. The settlers established several outposts and farms, including Fort Nya Elfsborg on the east bank of the river, near present-day Salem, New Jersey, and Fort Nya Gothenburg on Tinicum Island, which served as the residence of Governor Johan Printz. Printz, who arrived in 1643, was an energetic and authoritative leader who sought to consolidate and expand

Swedish control in the region. Under his administration, the colony saw the construction of additional fortifications, churches, and trading posts.

The presence of New Sweden, however, was a source of tension with the neighboring Dutch colony of New Netherland. The Dutch, headquartered in New Amsterdam (present-day New York City), viewed the Swedish settlement as an encroachment on their territory and a threat to their dominance in the fur trade. The Dutch West India Company, which controlled New Netherland, made several attempts to challenge Swedish claims and assert their authority over the Delaware Valley.

The geopolitical rivalry between the Swedes and the Dutch in the region came to a head in 1655. Peter Stuyvesant, the Director-General of New Netherland, launched a military expedition to conquer New Sweden. With a force of several hundred soldiers and a fleet of ships, Stuyvesant's campaign quickly overpowered the Swedish defenses. Fort Christina and other Swedish outposts were captured, and the colony was formally absorbed into New Netherland. The fall of New Sweden marked the end of Swedish political control in North America, but the settlers were allowed to remain and continue their way of life under Dutch rule.

Although the Swedish colonial venture in Delaware was short-lived, its impact was enduring. The Swedes and Finns who settled in the region left a lasting imprint on the cultural and social landscape. Their traditions, particularly in architecture, agriculture, and religion, persisted long after the colony's incorporation into New Netherland and later into the English colonies following the English conquest of New Netherland in 1664.

One of the most notable contributions of the Swedish settlers was the introduction of the log cabin to North America. This building technique, brought by the Finns, became a quintessential element of American frontier architecture. The log cabin provided a sturdy, simple, and effective solution for housing in the wilderness, and its design was widely adopted by settlers across the continent in subsequent centuries.

The religious heritage of New Sweden also had a lasting influence. The Swedish Lutheran Church established congregations and built churches, such as the Holy Trinity Church (Old Swedes') in Wilmington, which remains one of the oldest continuously used churches in the United States. The religious practices and institutions founded by the Swedish settlers contributed to the diverse religious landscape of early America.

In the broader context of North American colonial history, New Sweden represents an example of the dynamic and competitive nature of European colonization. The Swedish attempt to establish a foothold in the Delaware Valley, though ultimately unsuccessful in terms of political control, demonstrated the interconnectedness of European, Indigenous, and African peoples in the colonial enterprise. The interactions between these groups were complex and multifaceted, involving cooperation, conflict, and cultural exchange.

The legacy of New Sweden is commemorated in various ways today. Historical sites, museums, and cultural organizations in Delaware and the surrounding region preserve and interpret the history of the Swedish colony. Events such as Swedish Colonial Day celebrate the contributions of the early Swedish and Finnish settlers to American history. These commemorations highlight the diverse origins of the United States and the rich tapestry of its colonial past.

The Swedish colonization of Delaware was a brief but significant chapter in the history of European colonization in North America. Driven by economic and geopolitical ambitions, the Swedes established a small but thriving colony along the Delaware River, engaging in trade, agriculture, and cultural exchange with Indigenous peoples and other European settlers. Despite its eventual conquest by the Dutch, the legacy of New Sweden endured through the contributions of its settlers to American culture, architecture, and religious life. The story of New Sweden serves as a reminder of the diverse and interconnected nature of early colonial endeavors in the New World.

Chapter 37: Russian Colonization of Alaska

The Russian colonization of Alaska, an often overlooked yet significant episode in the history of North American colonization, began in the 18th century and continued until the mid-19th century. This period, marked by exploration, trade, and territorial expansion, ultimately led to Russia's sale of Alaska to the United States in 1867. The Russian presence in Alaska left an enduring legacy on the region's cultural, economic, and social landscape.

The origins of Russian interest in Alaska can be traced back to the ambitions of the Russian Empire under Peter the Great, who sought to expand his nation's influence and economic wealth through exploration and colonization. The initial motivation was the lucrative fur trade, particularly in sea otter pelts, which were highly prized in China. The Russian Far East, with its proximity to the North American continent, provided a launching point for expeditions into uncharted territories.

The first significant Russian expedition to Alaska was led by the Danish navigator Vitus Bering, who was commissioned by Peter the Great. In 1728, Bering sailed through what would later be named the Bering Strait, establishing that Asia and North America were separate landmasses. His second expedition in 1741, alongside Alexei Chirikov, resulted in the first recorded European sightings of the Alaskan mainland and the Aleutian Islands. Bering's voyages opened the door for Russian expansion into Alaska and laid the groundwork for future exploration and colonization.

Following Bering's expeditions, Russian fur traders, known as promyshlenniki, began to venture into Alaska in search of sea otter pelts. These traders established temporary camps and trading posts along the Aleutian Islands and the Alaskan mainland. The Russian fur trade was characterized by a highly exploitative relationship with the Indigenous populations, particularly the Aleuts, who were often coerced into hunting for the Russians. The promyshlenniki imposed harsh labor conditions and exacted tribute from the Aleuts in the form of furs, leading to significant disruptions in their traditional way of life.

In 1784, the first permanent Russian settlement in Alaska was established by Grigory Shelikhov on Kodiak Island. Shelikhov, a prominent fur trader, founded the Three Saints Bay colony, which served as a base for further expansion and exploitation of the region's fur resources. The settlement marked the beginning of formal Russian colonial administration in Alaska, and Shelikhov's company, the Shelikhov-Golikov Company, played a crucial role in consolidating Russian control over the territory.

The Russian-American Company (RAC), chartered by Tsar Paul I in 1799, became the primary instrument of Russian colonization in Alaska. The RAC was granted monopolistic control over the region's trade and governance, effectively making it an extension of the Russian state. Under the leadership of Alexander Baranov, the company's first chief manager, the RAC expanded its operations, establishing additional settlements and trading posts, including the prominent colony of New Archangel (Sitka) in 1804. New Archangel became the capital of Russian America and the center of administrative, commercial, and military activities.

The Russian colonization of Alaska was marked by a complex and often fraught relationship with the Indigenous populations. The Russians encountered a diverse array of Indigenous groups, including the Aleuts, Tlingit, Haida, and Yup'ik, each with their own distinct cultures, languages, and social structures. The fur trade and the establishment of Russian settlements led to significant cultural exchanges, intermarriage, and, at times, violent conflicts. The Tlingit, for example, resisted Russian encroachment on their lands, culminating in the Battle of Sitka in 1804, where Russian forces, with the aid of Aleut allies, defeated the Tlingit and secured control over the region.

The Russian colonial administration sought to integrate the Indigenous populations into the colonial economy through a system of tribute and labor. The RAC relied heavily on Indigenous labor for hunting, fishing, and other economic activities. Indigenous people were often coerced into providing labor and goods, and those who resisted were subjected to punitive measures. This exploitative system had devastating effects on Indigenous communities, leading to population decline, social disruption, and cultural loss.

Despite these challenges, there were also instances of cooperation and cultural exchange between Russians and Indigenous peoples. The Russian Orthodox Church played a significant role in this regard, establishing missions and schools to convert and educate Indigenous populations. The Church's efforts led to the spread of Orthodoxy among many Indigenous groups, who integrated elements of Russian religious practices with their own traditions. The legacy of Russian Orthodoxy remains evident in Alaska today, with numerous churches and communities maintaining the faith.

The economic foundation of Russian America was the fur trade, which experienced periods of boom and bust depending on market conditions and the availability of fur-bearing animals. The depletion of sea otter populations due to overhunting forced the RAC to diversify its economic activities. The company expanded into agriculture, fishing, and the production of goods such as bricks and lumber. However, the colony's remote location, harsh climate, and logistical challenges made these efforts difficult and often unprofitable.

The Russian presence in Alaska faced increasing challenges from other colonial powers, particularly the British and Americans, who were also interested in the region's resources. The British Hudson's Bay Company established trading posts and engaged in competition with the RAC for fur trade dominance. American traders and whalers also began to operate in Alaskan waters, further encroaching on Russian interests. These pressures, combined with internal issues such as mismanagement and corruption within the RAC, weakened Russian control over Alaska.

By the mid-19th century, the Russian Empire began to reassess its colonial ambitions in Alaska. The Crimean War (1853-1856) strained Russian resources and exposed the vulnerabilities of maintaining a distant and costly colony. The changing geopolitical landscape, coupled with the declining profitability of the fur trade, led Russian officials to consider the possibility of selling Alaska. The United States, expanding westward and eager to establish a presence in the Pacific, emerged as a potential buyer.

The negotiations for the sale of Alaska were conducted between the Russian Minister to the United States, Eduard de Stoeckl, and the American Secretary of State, William H. Seward. The two parties reached an agreement in 1867, with the United States purchasing Alaska for $7.2 million, a transaction that became known as "Seward's Folly" due to initial skepticism about the value of the acquisition. The transfer of sovereignty was formalized on October 18, 1867, with a ceremonial raising of the American flag in Sitka.

The legacy of Russian colonization in Alaska is multifaceted and enduring. The Russian influence is evident in the region's cultural, religious, and architectural heritage. Russian place names, such as Kodiak, Sitka, and Baranof Island, remain as reminders of the colonial period. The Russian Orthodox Church continues to play a significant role in Alaskan communities, with many Indigenous and non-Indigenous Alaskans practicing the faith. The historical interactions between Russians and Indigenous peoples have also left a lasting impact on the social fabric of the region.

The Russian colonial period in Alaska also had profound environmental and economic consequences. The intense exploitation of fur-bearing animals led to significant ecological changes, including the near-extinction of sea otters. The introduction of new technologies, goods, and agricultural practices by the Russians transformed Indigenous ways of life and altered the region's economic landscape. The legacy of these changes continues to shape the environmental and economic realities of contemporary Alaska.

The history of Russian colonization in Alaska provides valuable insights into the broader dynamics of European colonialism in North America. It highlights the complex interactions between colonizers and Indigenous populations, the economic motivations driving colonial expansion, and the geopolitical rivalries that shaped the continent's history. The Russian experience in Alaska, while distinct, shares commonalities with other colonial endeavors, underscoring the interconnectedness of global historical processes.

The Russian colonization of Alaska, though relatively brief in duration, left an indelible mark on the region. Driven by the pursuit of economic gain through the fur trade, Russian explorers, traders, and settlers established a network of settlements and trading posts that facilitated the exploitation of Alaskan resources. The interactions between Russians and Indigenous peoples were marked by both conflict and cooperation, leading to significant cultural exchanges and lasting impacts on Indigenous communities. The eventual sale of Alaska to the United States marked the end of Russian colonial ambitions in North America but did not erase the legacy of Russian influence in the region. Today, the history of Russian Alaska is commemorated through cultural institutions, historical sites, and the enduring presence of Russian heritage in Alaskan society.

Chapter 38: Spanish Missions in California

The Spanish missions in California, spanning from 1769 to 1833, are a significant chapter in the history of the region, representing a complex and multifaceted period of cultural, religious, and social transformation. These missions were established by Spanish Franciscan missionaries with the dual purpose of converting Indigenous peoples to Christianity and securing Spain's territorial claims in the face of competing European powers. The missions profoundly impacted California's Indigenous populations, economy, and cultural landscape, leaving a lasting legacy that continues to be studied and debated today.

The Spanish Crown's interest in California was initially driven by geopolitical considerations. In the mid-18th century, Spain faced increasing competition from other European powers, particularly Russia and Great Britain, which were expanding their influence along the Pacific coast of North America. To solidify its claims and prevent encroachment, Spain sought to establish a series of missions, presidios (military forts), and pueblos (civilian towns) along the coast. This strategy was part of a broader effort to consolidate Spanish control over its vast territories in the Americas.

The establishment of the California missions began with the arrival of Gaspar de Portolá and Franciscan missionary Junípero Serra in 1769. Serra, who would later be canonized as a saint, played a pivotal role in founding the mission system. His fervent dedication to the evangelization of Indigenous peoples and his leadership were instrumental in the establishment and expansion of the missions. The first mission, Mission San Diego de Alcalá, was founded in 1769 in present-day San Diego. This marked the beginning of a chain of 21 missions that would stretch from San Diego in the south to Sonoma in the north.

Each mission was strategically located near Indigenous villages and along El Camino Real (The Royal Road), a route that connected the missions and facilitated travel and communication. The missions were designed to be self-sufficient communities, with each consisting of a church, living quarters for the missionaries and Indigenous converts (known as neophytes), workshops, and agricultural facilities. The architecture of the missions reflected a blend of Spanish, Moorish, and Indigenous influences, characterized by adobe buildings, clay tile roofs, and distinctive bell towers.

The primary goal of the missions was to convert Indigenous peoples to Christianity and integrate them into Spanish colonial society. The Franciscan missionaries believed that the salvation of Indigenous souls could only be achieved through conversion to Catholicism and assimilation into Spanish culture. To this end, the missions sought to transform every aspect of Indigenous life, including religion, language, dress, and work habits. Indigenous peoples were baptized, given Christian names, and instructed in the Catholic faith. They were also taught Spanish and trained in various European trades and agricultural practices.

Life at the missions was highly regimented and structured. The daily routine for neophytes typically began with morning prayers and Mass, followed by a day of labor and instruction, and ending with evening prayers. The missions relied heavily on the labor of Indigenous converts for their economic sustainability. Neophytes worked in the fields, tending to crops and livestock, and in workshops, producing goods such as leather, textiles, and pottery. The agricultural output of the missions included wheat, barley, corn, grapes, and various fruits and vegetables. The missions also raised cattle, sheep, and other livestock, contributing to the development of California's ranching industry.

The impact of the missions on Indigenous populations was profound and often devastating. The introduction of European diseases, to which Indigenous peoples had no immunity, led to significant population decline. Epidemics of smallpox, measles, and other illnesses swept through the missions, decimating Indigenous communities. The harsh and unfamiliar labor conditions, coupled with the loss of traditional ways of life, further contributed to the suffering and dislocation of Indigenous peoples.

The missions also imposed strict discipline and control over the neophytes. Punishments for disobedience or attempts to escape were severe, including flogging, confinement, and other forms of corporal punishment. The coercive and authoritarian nature of mission life often led to resistance and rebellion among the Indigenous population. There were numerous instances of Indigenous uprisings and escapes, reflecting the deep resentment and resistance to the mission system.

Despite the oppressive conditions, the missions were also sites of significant cultural exchange and adaptation. Indigenous peoples brought their own skills, knowledge, and traditions to the mission environment, leading to the emergence of a unique blend of Spanish and Indigenous cultural practices. This syncretism was evident in various aspects of mission life, including music, art, cuisine, and religious practices. For example, Indigenous musical instruments and styles were incorporated into church services, and Indigenous artistic motifs appeared in mission art and architecture.

The mission system reached its zenith in the early 19th century, with thousands of Indigenous converts and extensive agricultural and economic production. However, the decline of the Spanish Empire and the political upheavals in Mexico, which gained independence from Spain in 1821, had a profound impact on the missions. The Mexican government viewed the missions with suspicion, associating them with Spanish colonial rule and ecclesiastical power. In 1833, the Mexican government enacted the secularization laws, which aimed to dismantle the mission system and redistribute mission lands to Indigenous peoples and Mexican settlers.

The process of secularization was fraught with challenges and complexities. Many missions were poorly managed during the transition, leading to the decline of agricultural production and economic instability. The redistribution of land often failed to benefit Indigenous communities, as much of the land ended up in the hands of private Mexican and later American landowners. The mission buildings themselves fell into disrepair, and the vibrant communities that had once thrived within their walls were largely dispersed.

The legacy of the California missions is a subject of ongoing debate and reflection. On one hand, the missions played a crucial role in the colonization and development of California, laying the foundations for the state's agricultural and economic growth. The missions also contributed to the spread of Christianity and the establishment of enduring cultural and religious institutions. The mission period left an indelible mark on California's cultural landscape, with mission architecture and place names still visible across the state.

On the other hand, the missions were sites of profound cultural disruption, exploitation, and violence against Indigenous peoples. The forced labor, harsh discipline, and cultural assimilation policies imposed by the missions had devastating effects on Indigenous communities, leading to significant loss of life, land, and cultural heritage. The mission period represents a painful and contentious chapter in the history of Indigenous peoples in California, and its legacy continues to be the subject of critical examination and reinterpretation.

Today, the California missions are preserved as historical landmarks and museums, attracting visitors from around the world. Efforts to restore and interpret the missions emphasize both their historical significance and the need to acknowledge and address the injustices and suffering experienced by Indigenous peoples. Educational programs, exhibitions, and public discussions aim to provide a more nuanced and inclusive understanding of the mission period, highlighting the diverse perspectives and experiences of those who lived through it.

The Spanish missions in California represent a complex and multifaceted period of cultural, religious, and social transformation. Established with the dual purpose of converting Indigenous peoples to Christianity and securing Spanish territorial claims, the missions profoundly impacted the region's Indigenous populations, economy, and cultural landscape. The legacy of the missions is a subject of ongoing debate and reflection, underscoring the need for a comprehensive and balanced understanding of this significant chapter in California's history.

Chapter 39: British Rule in Cyprus

British rule in Cyprus, which spanned from 1878 to 1960, represents a complex and multifaceted period in the island's history. This era saw significant political, social, and economic changes that have left a lasting impact on Cyprus. The British administration inherited a diverse and historically rich island that had been under Ottoman control since 1571. The strategic location of Cyprus in the eastern Mediterranean made it a valuable asset for the British Empire, particularly in the context of its imperial interests in the region.

The British occupation of Cyprus began as part of the geopolitical maneuvering during the late 19th century. In 1878, the British and Ottoman Empires signed the Cyprus Convention, which allowed Britain to occupy and administer Cyprus in exchange for promising to protect the Ottoman Empire against potential Russian aggression. This agreement was influenced by the larger context of the Great Game, the strategic rivalry between the British and Russian Empires. Cyprus's proximity to the Suez Canal, a critical maritime route to British India, added to its strategic importance.

Initially, Cyprus remained nominally part of the Ottoman Empire, but the British quickly established their administrative framework. The first High Commissioner, Sir Garnet Wolseley, oversaw the transition of power and set up the British colonial administration. The British sought to modernize the island's infrastructure and governance while maintaining a relatively light touch on the existing social and economic structures. This period was marked by efforts to improve public health, education, and agriculture, though these changes were often limited by financial constraints and the complexities of colonial governance.

One of the key aspects of British rule in Cyprus was the introduction of a modern legal and administrative system. The British established a legal framework based on British common law principles, which significantly differed from the Ottoman legal system that had been in place. This included the introduction of new land tenure laws, judicial reforms, and a more centralized administrative structure. These changes aimed to create a more efficient and predictable system of governance, although they often met with resistance from local communities who were accustomed to the Ottoman way of life.

The British administration also invested in infrastructure development, which had long-lasting impacts on the island's economy and society. They built roads, ports, and telegraph lines to improve communication and transportation across the island. These projects facilitated trade and mobility, contributing to economic growth. The British also implemented agricultural reforms, encouraging the cultivation of cash crops like carob, tobacco, and citrus fruits, which became important exports. These efforts aimed to integrate Cyprus more closely into the global economy and enhance its economic self-sufficiency.

Education was another area of focus for the British colonial authorities. They introduced a new education system based on the British model, which aimed to provide a more secular and standardized education. The British established public schools and encouraged the development of vocational and technical education to support economic development. However, the education system remained segregated along ethnic and religious lines, with separate schools for Greek Cypriots, Turkish Cypriots, and other minority communities. This segregation reflected and reinforced the existing divisions within Cypriot society.

The early years of British rule were characterized by relative stability, but tensions soon began to emerge. The Greek Cypriot population, which constituted the majority of the island's inhabitants, harbored aspirations for Enosis, or union with Greece. This sentiment was fueled by the broader nationalist movements sweeping across Europe and the Balkans. The Greek Orthodox Church, a powerful institution in Cypriot society, played a leading role in promoting the idea of Enosis. The British authorities were aware of these sentiments but were initially able to manage them through a combination of political concessions and repression.

The political landscape in Cyprus began to change more dramatically in the early 20th century. The 1931 Cyprus revolt, also known as the October Revolt, marked a turning point in the island's history. The revolt was sparked by widespread dissatisfaction with British rule, economic hardships, and the desire for greater political autonomy. It began as a series of protests and demonstrations but quickly escalated into violent clashes between Greek Cypriot protesters and British colonial forces. The British response was swift and harsh, with the imposition of martial law, mass arrests, and the deportation of key leaders.

In the aftermath of the revolt, the British authorities implemented a series of repressive measures aimed at quelling dissent and maintaining control. They dissolved the elected Legislative Council, which had provided a limited degree of political representation for Cypriots, and replaced it with a more authoritarian administrative structure. These measures deepened the divide between the British rulers and the Cypriot population, particularly among Greek Cypriots, who felt increasingly alienated and disenfranchised.

During World War II, Cyprus played a strategic role as a base for Allied operations in the Eastern Mediterranean. The island's strategic location made it a crucial point for supply lines and military operations. Many Cypriots enlisted in the British armed forces and contributed to the war effort, hoping that their loyalty would be rewarded with greater political rights and progress towards self-determination. However, the post-war period brought disappointment as the British were reluctant to grant significant political concessions.

The struggle for independence and self-determination intensified in the post-war years. The demand for Enosis grew stronger, with Greek

Cypriots increasingly frustrated by the lack of progress towards their goal. The formation of the National Organization of Cypriot Fighters (EOKA) in 1955 marked the beginning of an armed insurgency against British rule. Led by George Grivas, a former Greek army officer, EOKA launched a guerrilla campaign aimed at ending British colonial rule and achieving union with Greece. The insurgency involved a series of bombings, assassinations, and sabotage operations targeting British military installations, government buildings, and personnel. The British authorities responded with a counterinsurgency campaign, deploying thousands of troops to the island, imposing curfews, conducting mass arrests, and using harsh interrogation techniques.

The conflict between EOKA and British forces created a highly volatile and violent environment in Cyprus. The British employed a range of counterinsurgency tactics, including the use of informers, intelligence operations, and punitive measures against suspected insurgents and their supporters. The insurgency and the British response had a profound impact on Cypriot society, leading to widespread fear, suspicion, and division. The violence and repression further fueled anti-colonial sentiment among Greek Cypriots and intensified their demands for Enosis.

At the same time, the Turkish Cypriot community, which constituted a significant minority on the island, had different political aspirations. Fearing domination by the Greek Cypriot majority in the event of Enosis, Turkish Cypriots began to advocate for partition (Taksim) or a separate political status that would protect their interests. The British authorities, recognizing the potential for intercommunal conflict, sought to balance the competing demands of the two communities. This often involved playing the two sides against each other, exacerbating tensions and mistrust.

The struggle for independence and the complex interplay of Greek Cypriot and Turkish Cypriot aspirations led to a protracted and contentious political process. In the late 1950s, the British government, faced with mounting international pressure and the untenable costs of maintaining colonial rule in Cyprus, began to explore a political settlement. This culminated in the Zurich and London Agreements of 1959, which established the framework for the creation of an independent Republic of Cyprus.

The agreements, negotiated by representatives of the Greek and Turkish Cypriot communities, as well as the governments of Greece, Turkey, and the United Kingdom, laid out a power-sharing arrangement that sought to address the interests of both communities. The new constitution provided for a Greek Cypriot president and a Turkish Cypriot vice president, as well as a bicommunal legislature and government. Cyprus was to remain a member of the British Commonwealth, and Britain retained military bases on the island.

The Republic of Cyprus formally gained independence on August 16, 1960, ending 82 years of British colonial rule. However, the power-sharing arrangement and the constitutional framework established by the Zurich and London Agreements proved to be fragile. The inherent tensions and conflicting aspirations of the Greek and Turkish Cypriot communities soon resurfaced, leading to political instability and intercommunal violence in the early 1960s. The newly independent state faced numerous challenges, including the need to build a cohesive national identity, manage economic development, and navigate the complex geopolitics of the Eastern Mediterranean.

Despite the challenges and conflicts that followed independence, the British colonial period left a lasting legacy on Cyprus. The legal and administrative systems introduced by the British continued to influence the governance of the island. The infrastructure projects initiated during British rule laid the foundation for future economic development. The educational reforms, though imperfect, contributed to the growth of a more literate and skilled population.

Culturally, the British period in Cyprus was marked by a blend of influences. English became a widely spoken language, particularly in official and business contexts. British cultural institutions, such as schools, clubs, and sporting activities, left an imprint on Cypriot society. The island's legal system, administrative practices, and public institutions retained elements of British influence long after independence.

The history of British rule in Cyprus is a complex and contested narrative, reflecting the broader dynamics of colonialism, nationalism, and geopolitics. It is a story of economic and social transformation, cultural exchange, and political struggle. The legacy of British rule continues to be debated and reassessed, with historians, scholars, and the public exploring its multifaceted impacts on the island and its people.

The British colonial period in Cyprus, from 1878 to 1960, was marked by significant political, social, and economic changes that have left an enduring legacy on the island. Initially driven by geopolitical considerations, the British established a modern legal and administrative system, invested in infrastructure development, and introduced educational reforms. However, the period was also characterized by resistance and rebellion, particularly among the Greek Cypriot population, who aspired to union with Greece. The emergence of the armed insurgency led by EOKA in the 1950s, and the subsequent counterinsurgency campaign by the British, highlighted the deep divisions and tensions within Cypriot society. The eventual independence of Cyprus in 1960, following the Zurich and London Agreements, marked the end of British rule but did not resolve the underlying conflicts between the Greek and Turkish Cypriot communities. The legacy of British rule, encompassing both positive developments and significant challenges, continues to shape the history and identity of Cyprus.

Chapter 40: French Colonial Rule in Syria

French colonial rule in Syria, spanning from 1920 to 1946, represents a period of profound political, social, and economic transformation that left an indelible mark on the country. The mandate period, as it was officially known, was established under the auspices of the League of Nations following the defeat of the Ottoman Empire in World War I. The imposition of French control over Syria was met with resistance and unrest, as Syrians sought to assert their independence and define their national identity.

The origins of French involvement in Syria can be traced back to the Sykes-Picot Agreement of 1916, a secret treaty between Britain and France that outlined their respective spheres of influence in the Middle East following the anticipated collapse of the Ottoman Empire. Under this agreement, France was to gain control over modern-day Syria and Lebanon, while Britain would control Palestine, Transjordan, and Iraq. The agreement laid the groundwork for the division of the Ottoman territories into new political entities under European control.

Following the end of World War I, the League of Nations officially granted France the mandate for Syria and Lebanon in 1920. This decision was formalized at the San Remo Conference, which allocated the former Ottoman territories to the victorious Allied powers. The mandate system was ostensibly designed to prepare these territories for eventual self-governance, but in practice, it often served to entrench European colonial control.

The French mandate over Syria began with the military occupation of Damascus in July 1920, following the defeat of the short-lived Arab Kingdom of Syria, which had been established by Emir Faisal with the support of the British. The French quickly moved to consolidate their control, defeating Syrian forces at the Battle of Maysalun and establishing a colonial administration in Damascus. General Henri Gouraud, the French High Commissioner, oversaw the establishment of the mandate, implementing policies aimed at securing French interests and maintaining order.

One of the first actions taken by the French authorities was to divide Syria into several distinct administrative units, each with varying degrees of autonomy. This policy of divide and rule was designed to weaken nationalist movements and prevent the emergence of a unified opposition to French rule. The territory was divided into the State of Damascus, the State of Aleppo, the Alawite State, the Jabal Druze State, and the autonomous Sanjak of Alexandretta. Additionally, Lebanon was separated from Syria and established as a separate mandate, further fragmenting the region.

The French administration implemented a range of policies aimed at modernizing Syria's infrastructure and economy, as well as promoting French cultural and educational influence. They invested in the construction of roads, railways, and ports to facilitate trade and military movement. Urban centers such as Damascus and Aleppo saw the development of new public buildings, schools, and hospitals. The French also sought to introduce modern agricultural techniques and promote the cultivation of cash crops, such as cotton and tobacco, to integrate Syria more closely into the global economy.

Education was a key focus of French colonial policy, with the aim of fostering a Francophone elite loyal to French interests. French-language schools were established, and the curriculum emphasized French history, literature, and values. However, this educational policy was often met with resistance from Syrians, who sought to preserve their own cultural and linguistic heritage. Despite the French efforts, a significant portion of the population remained committed to Arabic language and culture, and the educational system became a battleground for competing nationalist and colonial ideologies.

The French mandate was characterized by frequent and often violent resistance from various segments of Syrian society. The most significant uprising against French rule occurred in 1925, known as the Great Syrian Revolt. This nationwide rebellion was led by a diverse coalition of nationalist groups, including Druze, Sunni, and Christian factions, united by their opposition to French control. The revolt began in the Jabal Druze region under the leadership of Sultan al-Atrash and quickly spread to other parts of Syria, including Damascus and Aleppo. The French responded with a brutal crackdown, employing heavy artillery and aerial bombardments to suppress the rebellion. The revolt was eventually quelled by 1927, but it left a lasting legacy of resistance and martyrdom in Syrian national memory.

Despite the suppression of the Great Syrian Revolt, nationalist sentiment continued to grow throughout the 1930s and 1940s. The emergence of political parties, such as the National Bloc, which advocated for independence and self-governance, reflected the increasing political mobilization of the Syrian population. The National Bloc, led by prominent figures like Hashim al-Atassi and Shukri al-Quwatli, sought to negotiate with the French for greater autonomy and ultimately, independence. These negotiations resulted in the Franco-Syrian Treaty of 1936, which promised gradual independence for Syria within three years. However, the treaty was never ratified by the French government, leading to widespread disappointment and further unrest.

The outbreak of World War II and the subsequent Vichy regime's control over Syria added another layer of complexity to the mandate period. In 1941, the Free French forces, with the support of the British, launched a campaign to wrest control of Syria from the Vichy government. This campaign, known as the Syria-Lebanon Campaign, resulted in the establishment of a Free French administration under General Georges Catroux, who promised eventual independence for

Syria and Lebanon. Despite these assurances, the road to independence remained fraught with challenges.

The post-war period saw renewed efforts by Syrian nationalists to achieve independence. The weakened state of France following World War II, combined with growing international pressure for decolonization, created a more favorable environment for Syrian aspirations. In 1945, Syria was admitted to the United Nations, signaling its growing international recognition as a sovereign state. The following year, negotiations between Syrian leaders and the French government culminated in the withdrawal of French troops and the official end of the mandate.

On April 17, 1946, Syria officially gained its independence, marking the end of 26 years of French colonial rule. The legacy of the mandate period, however, continued to shape the newly independent state. The administrative divisions and sectarian policies implemented by the French had lasting impacts on Syrian society, contributing to the complex interplay of ethnic, religious, and regional identities that would continue to influence Syrian politics. The infrastructure and educational systems established during the mandate period also provided a foundation for the new state's development, despite the challenges of post-colonial nation-building.

The French colonial rule in Syria, while often characterized by repression and resistance, also saw significant developments in infrastructure, education, and economic integration. The mandate period was marked by a complex interplay of colonial and nationalist forces, as Syrians navigated the challenges of foreign rule and sought to assert their own identity and sovereignty. The legacy of this period remains a critical part of Syrian history, reflecting the broader dynamics of colonialism and the struggle for independence in the 20th century.

Chapter 41: Dutch Colonization of New York

The Dutch colonization of what is now New York is a fascinating chapter in the history of North America, marked by economic ambition, cultural exchange, conflict, and eventual transition to English control. The Dutch presence in the region began in the early 17th century and lasted until 1664, but its legacy continues to influence the area to this day.

The story of Dutch colonization in New York begins with the exploration of Henry Hudson, an Englishman employed by the Dutch East India Company. In 1609, Hudson sailed his ship, the Halve Maen (Half Moon), up the river that would later bear his name. His journey laid the groundwork for Dutch claims to the region. Hudson's voyage revealed the potential for trade, particularly in furs, which were highly valued in Europe.

Following Hudson's exploration, the Dutch established the New Netherland colony, focusing on the lucrative fur trade with the Indigenous peoples of the region. The Dutch West India Company, founded in 1621, was granted a monopoly over this territory. The company's primary goal was to exploit the area's resources for profit, and it encouraged settlement to support this endeavor.

The first significant settlement was established in 1624 on Governors Island, but it was soon relocated to the southern tip of Manhattan. This new settlement, named New Amsterdam, became the administrative and commercial center of New Netherland. Under the leadership of the colony's first director, Peter Minuit, the Dutch famously purchased Manhattan Island from the local Lenape people in 1626 for goods valued at 60 guilders. While the transaction has often been mythologized as a shrewd and inexpensive purchase, it represented a fundamental misunderstanding between the Europeans and the Indigenous inhabitants, who had different concepts of land ownership and use.

The early years of New Amsterdam were challenging, marked by harsh living conditions, conflicts with Indigenous peoples, and economic difficulties. However, the colony gradually grew, attracting settlers from various backgrounds, including the Netherlands, other parts of Europe, and even Africa. The Dutch practice of religious tolerance allowed for a diverse and cosmopolitan population. This policy, combined with the economic opportunities in the New World, drew Jews, French Huguenots, and other persecuted groups seeking refuge.

The Dutch West India Company implemented a patroon system to encourage colonization. Wealthy individuals, known as patroons, were granted large tracts of land along the Hudson River if they could establish settlements of at least 50 people within four years. This system led to the creation of several large estates, most notably Rensselaerswyck, near present-day Albany, managed by the powerful Van Rensselaer family. These estates operated like feudal manors, with tenant farmers working the land under the control of the patroons.

Relations with Indigenous peoples were complex and often strained. Initially, the Dutch engaged in trade with the local tribes, exchanging European goods for beaver pelts. However, competition for resources and differing cultural practices led to conflicts. One of the most significant confrontations was Kieft's War (1643-1645), named after Director Willem Kieft, who attempted to impose taxes on the Indigenous populations and launched brutal military campaigns against them. The resulting violence devastated both the Dutch and the Indigenous communities and highlighted the colony's fragile stability.

Under the leadership of Peter Stuyvesant, who became director-general in 1647, New Netherland saw significant development. Stuyvesant, a staunch and sometimes authoritarian leader, implemented various reforms to improve the colony's defenses, infrastructure, and governance. He expanded New Amsterdam's fortifications, established a formal market, and improved the colony's legal and administrative systems. Stuyvesant's tenure was marked by efforts to strengthen the colony's economy and ensure its survival in a competitive and often hostile environment.

Despite these efforts, New Netherland faced external threats from rival European powers, particularly the English. The English colonies in New England and the Chesapeake Bay were expanding, and tensions between the Dutch and English settlers were frequent. The strategic location of New Netherland, controlling access to the Hudson River and the fertile lands of the interior, made it a desirable target for English ambitions.

In 1664, during the Second Anglo-Dutch War, an English fleet led by Colonel Richard Nicolls sailed into New Amsterdam's harbor. Outnumbered and unprepared for a prolonged defense, Stuyvesant reluctantly surrendered the colony without a fight. The English renamed the settlement New York, in honor of the Duke of York, the future King James II, who had been granted the territory by his brother, King Charles II. This transfer marked the end of Dutch political control, but the Dutch influence persisted in various aspects of the region's culture, economy, and society.

Under English rule, New York continued to grow and prosper. The English maintained many of the Dutch legal practices and landholding systems, recognizing their effectiveness and the entrenched interests of the colony's inhabitants. The diverse population, established during the Dutch period, continued to thrive, contributing to New York's reputation as a melting pot of cultures and ideas. The city's strategic location and thriving port facilitated its development into a major commercial and trading hub.

The legacy of Dutch colonization in New York is evident in various aspects of the region's culture and heritage. Dutch place names, such as Harlem, Brooklyn (from Breuckelen), and Flushing (from Vlissingen), are still in use today. The influence of Dutch architecture can be seen in the gabled roofs and brick houses that remain in some areas. Dutch customs and traditions, such as St. Nicholas celebrations, evolved into uniquely American practices like Santa Claus.

The Dutch Reformed Church played a significant role in the religious and social life of the colony, and its legacy persists in the Reformed Church in America. The Dutch language continued to be spoken by some communities well into the 18th century, contributing to the linguistic diversity of the region. The patroon system, although it eventually declined, set a precedent for large landholdings and the development of agrarian estates in the Hudson Valley.

Chapter 42: Portuguese Presence in Mozambique

The Portuguese presence in Mozambique is a complex and multifaceted history that spans over four centuries, marked by exploration, colonization, economic exploitation, cultural exchange, resistance, and eventual independence. The Portuguese first arrived in the region in the late 15th century during their Age of Exploration, seeking new trade routes and opportunities. This long period of interaction has left a profound impact on Mozambique's development and its position within the broader context of African and world history.

The initial Portuguese exploration of the East African coast was part of a broader maritime strategy to establish a sea route to India and the spice markets of Asia. In 1498, the Portuguese navigator Vasco da Gama reached the coast of Mozambique, and this marked the beginning of Portuguese involvement in the region. Da Gama's voyage was significant not only for its navigational achievements but also for initiating a period of Portuguese influence along the Swahili Coast, which was already a hub of trade networks connecting Africa, the Middle East, and Asia.

The Portuguese initially established a series of fortified trading posts and settlements along the coast. They aimed to control the lucrative trade in gold, ivory, and slaves, which had been flourishing for centuries under the control of Arab and Swahili merchants. Notable among these early settlements was the island of Mozambique, which became the capital of Portuguese East Africa. The fortresses and churches built during this period, such as the Fort of São Sebastião and the Chapel of Nossa Senhora de Baluarte, reflect the early Portuguese architectural influence and their intent to secure and dominate the regional trade.

Throughout the 16th and 17th centuries, the Portuguese expanded their influence inland, establishing relations with local African rulers and engaging in various forms of economic activity, including agriculture, mining, and trade. However, their inland penetration was often met with resistance from local communities. The Portuguese relied heavily on alliances with local chieftains and the strategic placement of fortified settlements to maintain their presence.

The colonization process was further complicated by the emergence of the Zambezi prazos system in the 17th century. Prazos were large land grants given to Portuguese settlers, who operated as semi-autonomous feudal lords, often ruling over vast territories and significant numbers of African subjects. These prazos became centers of agricultural production, trade, and the slave economy. The prazo holders, or prazeiros, maintained their own private armies and operated with considerable independence from the colonial authorities, leading to a fragmented and often unstable colonial administration.

The economic activities during this period were varied and included the export of gold, ivory, and slaves. The slave trade, in particular, became a significant and tragic part of Mozambique's history. The Portuguese and their local allies captured and exported large numbers of Africans to work in plantations and mines in Brazil, the Caribbean, and other parts of the Portuguese Empire. This trade had devastating effects on the local population, leading to social disruption, depopulation, and the erosion of traditional societies.

The Portuguese influence in Mozambique experienced fluctuations in intensity and control. In the late 18th and early 19th centuries, Portuguese authority waned due to internal strife, competition from other European powers, and the growing resistance from local African states. The rise of the powerful Zulu kingdom to the south and the Ngoni migrations in the interior also posed significant challenges to

Portuguese control. The situation further deteriorated with the arrival of British and French colonial ambitions in the region.

In the mid-19th century, the Portuguese attempted to reassert their control over Mozambique by launching military campaigns to suppress local resistance and by negotiating boundaries with other colonial powers through a series of treaties. The Berlin Conference of 1884-1885, which formalized the Scramble for Africa, recognized Portugal's claim to Mozambique but also intensified European competition in the region.

The late 19th and early 20th centuries saw a renewed effort by the Portuguese to consolidate their colonial administration and exploit the economic potential of Mozambique. This period was marked by the establishment of more direct colonial rule, infrastructural development, and the integration of Mozambique into the global capitalist economy. The construction of railways, ports, and roads facilitated the export of agricultural and mineral resources, including cotton, tea, sugar, and coal.

However, the imposition of colonial rule and economic exploitation led to widespread discontent among the African population. The colonial administration imposed harsh labor policies, including forced labor (chibalo), high taxes, and land expropriation, which exacerbated poverty and social inequality. The growing resentment against these policies laid the groundwork for future resistance movements.

The early 20th century also saw the rise of nationalist sentiments and the formation of movements advocating for the rights and self-determination of the African population. The influence of global anti-colonial movements, coupled with the oppressive conditions under Portuguese rule, inspired many Mozambicans to seek change. Political consciousness was further enhanced by the activities of educated elites, labor migrants, and ex-servicemen who had been exposed to different political ideologies abroad.

The mid-20th century was a period of significant political and social upheaval in Mozambique. The decolonization wave that swept across Africa after World War II had a profound impact on Mozambique. In 1962, the Front for the Liberation of Mozambique (FRELIMO) was founded under the leadership of Eduardo Mondlane. FRELIMO united various nationalist factions and launched an armed struggle against Portuguese colonial rule in 1964. The guerrilla warfare campaign was centered in the northern provinces of Cabo Delgado and Niassa and received support from neighboring African countries and socialist bloc nations.

The Mozambican War of Independence lasted for a decade, marked by fierce fighting, significant casualties, and widespread destruction. FRELIMO's strategy combined military operations with efforts to mobilize and politicize the rural population, establishing liberated zones where they implemented social and economic reforms. The war placed a considerable strain on Portugal's resources and contributed to the political instability that led to the Carnation Revolution in Portugal in 1974.

The Carnation Revolution, a peaceful coup by the Portuguese military, overthrew the Estado Novo regime and led to a rapid decolonization process. In September 1974, Portugal and FRELIMO signed the Lusaka Accord, which laid the groundwork for Mozambique's independence. On June 25, 1975, Mozambique officially gained independence, with FRELIMO forming the new government under President Samora Machel.

Post-independence Mozambique faced numerous challenges, including rebuilding a war-torn country, addressing the legacy of colonialism, and navigating Cold War geopolitics. FRELIMO adopted Marxist-Leninist policies and sought to transform Mozambique into a socialist state. The new government nationalized key industries, implemented land reforms, and prioritized education and healthcare.

However, these policies were met with internal opposition and external interference.

One of the most significant post-independence challenges was the Mozambican Civil War, which began in 1977 and lasted until 1992. The conflict pitted the FRELIMO government against the Mozambican National Resistance (RENAMO), a rebel group initially supported by Rhodesia (now Zimbabwe) and later by apartheid South Africa. The civil war caused immense suffering, with widespread displacement, economic collapse, and human rights abuses.

The civil war ended with the Rome General Peace Accords in 1992, leading to a period of reconstruction and democratization. Mozambique transitioned to a multi-party democracy, with the first multi-party elections held in 1994. Despite significant progress in political stability and economic growth, Mozambique continues to face challenges related to poverty, inequality, and political tensions.

The Portuguese legacy in Mozambique is evident in various aspects of the country's culture, language, and social structures. Portuguese is the official language and serves as a lingua franca in a nation with diverse ethnic and linguistic groups. The legal and educational systems also reflect Portuguese influence, and many Mozambicans of mixed African and Portuguese heritage (mestiços) continue to play important roles in society.

Chapter 43: German Rule in Cameroon

German rule in Cameroon, spanning from 1884 to 1916, represents a significant yet often overlooked chapter in the history of both Germany and Africa. This period was marked by economic exploitation, infrastructural development, cultural imposition, resistance, and significant transformation of Cameroonian society. The German colonization of Cameroon, part of the broader Scramble for Africa, left an indelible legacy that continued to influence the country long after the end of German rule.

The beginnings of German interest in Cameroon can be traced to the mid-19th century, when German traders and missionaries started establishing a presence along the West African coast. By the early 1880s, the region was already attracting the attention of European powers eager to expand their colonial territories. In 1884, under the leadership of Chancellor Otto von Bismarck, Germany formally established a protectorate over Cameroon. This move was part of Germany's broader strategy to assert itself as a colonial power and compete with other European nations, particularly Britain and France, for influence and resources in Africa.

The official establishment of the German protectorate was marked by the signing of treaties with local chiefs, who, often under duress or misunderstanding, ceded their sovereignty in exchange for protection and economic benefits. These treaties laid the groundwork for German administration, with the coastal town of Douala becoming the colony's administrative center. The initial years of German rule focused on consolidating control over the territory, which involved both negotiation and military action to subdue resistance from local groups.

The German colonial administration in Cameroon, led by Governor Julius von Soden and later by others, embarked on an ambitious program of economic exploitation and infrastructural development. The primary objective was to make the colony economically self-sufficient and profitable for the German Empire. To achieve this, the Germans focused on developing plantations for cash crops such as cocoa, coffee, rubber, and bananas. Large tracts of land were expropriated from local communities and allocated to German settlers and companies, leading to significant displacement and disruption of traditional agricultural practices.

The plantation economy relied heavily on forced labor, which became a cornerstone of German colonial policy. Indigenous Cameroonians were coerced into working on plantations under harsh conditions, often with little regard for their well-being. The forced labor system, known as "corvée," required locals to perform mandatory work for the colonial administration or face severe punishment. This exploitative system caused widespread suffering and resentment among the population, contributing to tensions and resistance.

In addition to plantations, the Germans invested in the development of infrastructure to facilitate the extraction and export of resources. The construction of railways, roads, and ports was prioritized to connect the interior regions with the coast. Notable infrastructure projects included the Northern Railway, which connected the inland town of Yaoundé with the coastal city of Douala, and the port of Douala, which became a major hub for the export of agricultural products. These developments significantly altered the landscape and economy of Cameroon, integrating it more closely into the global capitalist system.

German rule also brought about significant changes in the social and cultural fabric of Cameroonian society. The colonial administration implemented policies aimed at transforming indigenous social structures and imposing European norms and values. Christian missionary activity was encouraged and supported by the colonial government, leading to the establishment of mission schools and churches. These missions played a dual role in promoting

Christianity and providing basic education, albeit with a strong emphasis on European cultural assimilation.

The introduction of Western education, though limited in scope, had a profound impact on Cameroonian society. Mission schools taught reading, writing, and arithmetic, alongside religious instruction, creating a small but growing educated elite. This educated class would later play a crucial role in the nationalist movements that emerged in the mid-20th century. However, the educational opportunities were often restricted to a few, and the majority of the population remained excluded from formal education and its potential benefits.

Resistance to German rule was a constant feature throughout the colonial period. Various ethnic groups and communities resisted German encroachment on their lands and the imposition of colonial policies. One of the most significant uprisings was led by the Duala people in the coastal region. King Rudolf Duala Manga Bell and other leaders opposed the expropriation of their lands and the oppressive labor practices. Their resistance culminated in the execution of King Bell by the German authorities in 1914, an event that underscored the brutal repression of dissent.

Another notable resistance movement was the uprising of the Bafut and Bali peoples in the northwest region. These groups resisted German attempts to impose direct rule and disrupt their traditional governance structures. The Germans responded with military expeditions that resulted in significant loss of life and destruction of property. Despite these setbacks, resistance persisted in various forms, reflecting the resilience and determination of the Cameroonian people to protect their autonomy and way of life.

The outbreak of World War I in 1914 marked a turning point for German rule in Cameroon. The war diverted German resources and attention away from their colonies, and the Allied powers, particularly Britain and France, saw an opportunity to seize German territories in Africa. In 1916, after a prolonged military campaign, German forces in Cameroon were defeated by a combined British and French expeditionary force. The defeat led to the partition of Cameroon between Britain and France under the Treaty of Versailles in 1919, officially ending German colonial rule.

The end of German rule did not erase its legacy in Cameroon. The infrastructure and economic structures established during the colonial period continued to shape the country's development under British and French administration. The forced labor practices and land expropriation policies had lasting social and economic impacts, contributing to patterns of inequality and exploitation that persisted into the post-colonial era. The introduction of Western education and Christianity also left a lasting imprint on Cameroonian culture and society.

In the post-independence period, Cameroon has grappled with the complex legacy of its colonial past. The dual heritage of British and French colonial rule has created a unique set of challenges and opportunities for nation-building. The country's bilingualism, with English and French as official languages, reflects this colonial history and presents both a unifying and divisive factor in national identity. The struggle for independence and the subsequent efforts to build a cohesive national identity have been influenced by the need to reconcile these diverse colonial legacies.

The memory of German rule, while often overshadowed by the more recent British and French periods, remains an important part of Cameroon's historical consciousness. The monuments, buildings, and place names from the German era serve as reminders of this chapter in the country's history. Scholarly research and public discourse continue to explore the complexities of German colonialism in Cameroon, contributing to a deeper understanding of its impacts and legacies.

Chapter 44: British Control of Malaya

The British control of Malaya is a profound and complex narrative that spans from the early 19th century until the mid-20th century. This period was characterized by political maneuvering, economic transformation, cultural exchange, social upheaval, and ultimately, the struggle for independence. The British presence in Malaya reshaped the region's demographics, infrastructure, and governance structures, leaving an enduring legacy that continues to influence modern Malaysia.

British interest in the Malay Peninsula can be traced back to the late 18th century, driven by the strategic location of the region along the maritime trade routes between India, China, and the wider Southeast Asian archipelago. The British East India Company (EIC) sought to secure a foothold in the region to protect its lucrative trade interests, particularly in spices and other valuable commodities. The establishment of Penang in 1786, by Captain Francis Light, marked the beginning of British territorial acquisitions in Malaya. Penang, located on the northwest coast of the peninsula, became a key trading post and naval base, laying the groundwork for further British expansion.

The early 19th century saw increased British involvement in Malaya, driven by both economic and strategic considerations. The signing of the Anglo-Dutch Treaty in 1824 was a pivotal moment, as it divided the Malay Archipelago into British and Dutch spheres of influence. Under the treaty, the British gained control of Malaya and Singapore, while the Dutch retained control of the Indonesian archipelago. This agreement facilitated the consolidation of British influence in the Malay Peninsula and set the stage for further expansion.

In 1826, the British established the Straits Settlements, a grouping of Penang, Malacca, and Singapore, under the administration of the EIC. The Straits Settlements became a crucial center for British trade and administration in the region. Singapore, in particular, flourished under British rule, rapidly transforming into a major port and commercial hub due to its strategic location and free port status. The growth of Singapore attracted traders and immigrants from China, India, and other parts of Asia, contributing to the multicultural fabric of the colony.

The mid-19th century marked a period of significant political and economic change in the Malay Peninsula. The discovery of tin deposits in the interior regions, particularly in Perak and Selangor, spurred a tin mining boom that attracted both British investment and Chinese labor. The influx of Chinese laborers, often organized into secret societies, led to increased social tensions and conflicts over control of the lucrative tin mines. These conflicts, known as the Larut Wars in Perak and the Klang War in Selangor, destabilized the region and prompted British intervention.

In response to the growing disorder and the economic importance of the tin industry, the British implemented a policy of indirect rule through the appointment of British Residents in the Malay states. This system, formalized by the Pangkor Treaty of 1874, placed British advisers in key positions to oversee the administration and economic development of the Malay states. The Residents exerted significant influence over local rulers, effectively reducing their sovereignty and integrating the Malay states into the British colonial framework. The establishment of the Federated Malay States (FMS) in 1896, comprising Perak, Selangor, Negeri Sembilan, and Pahang, further centralized British control and facilitated coordinated economic development.

The economic transformation of Malaya under British rule was profound, driven by the expansion of the tin and rubber industries. British investments in infrastructure, including railways, roads, and ports, facilitated the extraction and export of these commodities. The growth of the rubber industry, in particular, had a transformative impact on the Malayan economy. British planters introduced rubber cultivation in the late 19th century, and by the early 20th century, Malaya had become the world's leading producer of rubber. The demand for rubber, fueled by the automobile industry, created significant wealth for British investors and transformed the landscape of the peninsula, with vast plantations replacing traditional agricultural practices.

The development of the plantation economy had significant social and demographic implications. The need for labor in the tin mines and rubber plantations led to large-scale migration from China and India. The Chinese primarily worked in the tin mines and as traders, while the Indians were brought in as indentured laborers for the rubber plantations. This influx of migrants reshaped the demographic composition of Malaya, creating a plural society with distinct ethnic communities. The British colonial administration implemented policies to manage and control these diverse populations, often reinforcing ethnic divisions and hierarchies.

The social and economic changes brought about by British rule were accompanied by significant cultural and educational developments. The British established English-language schools and promoted Western education, primarily for the children of the elite and urban populations. Missionary schools also played a role in providing education, particularly to the Chinese and Indian communities. The introduction of Western education created a new class of educated Malaysians who would later play crucial roles in the nationalist movements of the mid-20th century.

The impact of British colonial policies on the indigenous Malay population was mixed. On one hand, the British protected the traditional privileges of the Malay rulers and maintained the Malay sultanates, ensuring their cooperation in the colonial administration. On the other hand, the economic benefits of British rule were unevenly distributed, with the Malay peasantry often remaining marginalized and excluded from the prosperity enjoyed by other ethnic communities. The British emphasis on maintaining the traditional Malay social structure also limited opportunities for upward mobility among the Malays.

The early 20th century saw the rise of nationalist sentiments and movements across Malaya. The growing awareness of global political changes, the impact of Western education, and the economic inequalities created by colonial policies all contributed to the emergence of nationalist ideologies. The formation of political organizations such as the Kesatuan Melayu Muda (KMM) in the 1930s reflected the growing discontent among the Malay population and their desire for greater political representation and independence. The influence of international events, including the decline of European colonial powers after World War I and the rise of anti-colonial movements in other parts of Asia, further fueled the nationalist fervor in Malaya.

The Japanese occupation of Malaya during World War II was a turning point in the history of British rule. The swift defeat of British forces and the harsh occupation by the Japanese military shattered the myth of British invincibility and exposed the vulnerabilities of colonial rule. The Japanese occupation, though brutal, also stimulated nationalist sentiments by undermining the colonial order and promoting anti-colonial propaganda. The Japanese encouraged Malay nationalism and attempted to win support from the local population, although their policies of forced labor and repression ultimately alienated many.

After the defeat of Japan in 1945, the British sought to reestablish their control over Malaya. However, the post-war period was marked by significant political and social upheaval. The British faced growing demands for independence from various ethnic and political groups. The Malayan Communist Party (MCP), which had fought against the Japanese occupation, now turned its efforts towards opposing British colonial rule, leading to the Malayan Emergency (1948-1960). The MCP's guerrilla warfare campaign posed a serious challenge to British authority and highlighted the widespread discontent with colonial rule.

In response to the growing unrest, the British implemented political reforms aimed at preparing Malaya for eventual self-governance. The establishment of the Federation of Malaya in 1948 marked a significant step towards independence, uniting the Malay states and the Straits Settlements (excluding Singapore) under a single political entity. The British introduced measures to promote economic development, improve social services, and expand political representation. However, these reforms were often seen as insufficient by the nationalist movements, who continued to press for full independence.

The path to independence was shaped by negotiations and compromises among the various ethnic and political groups in Malaya. The Alliance Party, formed in 1952 by the United Malays National Organisation (UMNO), the Malayan Chinese Association (MCA), and the Malayan Indian Congress (MIC), played a crucial role in advocating for independence. The Alliance Party's commitment to inter-ethnic cooperation and its ability to present a united front were instrumental in the negotiations with the British.

On August 31, 1957, the Federation of Malaya gained independence from Britain, with Tunku Abdul Rahman becoming the first Prime Minister. The achievement of independence was the culmination of decades of struggle and negotiation, reflecting the aspirations of the Malayan people for self-determination and sovereignty. The formation of Malaysia in 1963, which included Malaya, Singapore, Sabah, and Sarawak, further consolidated the nation's independence, although Singapore would later secede in 1965.

The legacy of British control in Malaya is multifaceted, encompassing both positive and negative aspects. The British left behind a well-developed infrastructure, including roads, railways, ports, and educational institutions, which laid the foundation for Malaya's post-independence economic development. The introduction of modern administrative and legal systems also contributed to the governance structures of the newly independent nation.

However, the social and economic inequalities created by colonial policies continued to pose challenges for independent Malaysia. The ethnic divisions and hierarchies reinforced by the British created a legacy of communalism that required careful management in the post-independence period. The need to address the disparities between the different ethnic communities, particularly the economic marginalization of the Malays, became a central focus of Malaysia's national policies.

Chapter 45: French Influence in Tunisia

French influence in Tunisia, spanning from the late 19th century to the mid-20th century, is a significant chapter in the history of North Africa. This period was marked by economic transformation, cultural assimilation, political change, social upheaval, and a gradual path towards independence. The impact of French colonization on Tunisia is profound and multifaceted, leaving a legacy that continues to shape the country's contemporary identity, politics, and society.

French interest in Tunisia began to manifest in the early 19th century, driven by a combination of strategic, economic, and political factors. The strategic location of Tunisia, situated along the Mediterranean Sea and in close proximity to the Italian peninsula, made it a coveted territory for European powers seeking to expand their influence in North Africa. Additionally, Tunisia's relatively weak political structure, coupled with its economic potential, made it an attractive target for French colonial ambitions.

The formal establishment of French control over Tunisia began with the signing of the Treaty of Bardo in 1881. This treaty, imposed on the ruling Bey of Tunisia, Sadok Bey, effectively placed Tunisia under French protectorate status. The treaty allowed the Bey to retain nominal authority, but real power was vested in the hands of the French Resident-General. This arrangement marked the beginning of a dual system of governance, where the traditional Tunisian administration coexisted with the French colonial administration, often leading to tensions and conflicts of interest.

The initial years of French rule focused on consolidating control over the territory and implementing economic and administrative reforms. The French administration embarked on a series of infrastructure projects aimed at modernizing Tunisia's economy and integrating it into the broader French colonial framework. These projects included the construction of railways, roads, ports, and telecommunication networks, which facilitated the movement of goods, people, and information. The development of the port of Tunis and the establishment of new towns and cities were particularly significant in transforming the economic landscape of Tunisia.

Economic exploitation was a central feature of French colonial policy in Tunisia. The French administration prioritized the extraction of resources and the development of agriculture, particularly the cultivation of cash crops such as olives, grapes, and cereals. Large tracts of land were expropriated from local communities and allocated to French settlers and investors, leading to significant displacement and disruption of traditional agricultural practices. The introduction of modern agricultural techniques and the expansion of irrigation systems increased agricultural productivity, but the benefits were unevenly distributed, with French settlers and a small elite class reaping the majority of the rewards.

The expansion of agriculture and resource extraction was accompanied by the development of industrial and commercial enterprises. The French established various industries, including mining, manufacturing, and processing, to exploit Tunisia's natural resources. The phosphate mines of Gafsa, in particular, became a major source of revenue for the French colonial administration. The growth of these industries attracted foreign investment and labor, further transforming the economic and social fabric of Tunisia.

The economic changes brought about by French rule had significant social implications. The influx of French settlers and the establishment of European-style businesses and institutions created a distinct colonial society, characterized by a sharp divide between the European elite and the indigenous Tunisian population. The colonial administration implemented policies that favored Europeans in employment, education, and access to resources, exacerbating social inequalities and fostering resentment among Tunisians. The development of urban centers, such as Tunis, Sfax, and Bizerte, led to the growth of a diverse and cosmopolitan population, but also highlighted the disparities between the colonial and indigenous communities.

Cultural assimilation was another key aspect of French colonial policy in Tunisia. The French administration sought to impose French language, culture, and values on the Tunisian population through the education system, media, and public institutions. French was established as the official language of administration, education, and commerce, and French cultural norms were promoted in schools and public life. The establishment of French-language schools, both secular and missionary, aimed to educate a new generation of Tunisians who would be loyal to the colonial regime and adopt French cultural values.

The introduction of Western education had a profound impact on Tunisian society, creating a small but growing educated elite. This educated class, known as the évolués, often found themselves caught between the traditional values of their own culture and the modern ideals promoted by the French. While some embraced the opportunities provided by Western education and sought to integrate into the colonial administration or business world, others became increasingly aware of the contradictions and injustices of colonial rule. This awareness would later fuel the nationalist movements that emerged in the mid-20th century.

Resistance to French rule was a constant undercurrent throughout the colonial period. Various forms of resistance, ranging from passive non-cooperation to active rebellion, characterized the relationship between the colonizers and the colonized. The early years of French rule saw sporadic uprisings and protests, often led by local leaders who resisted the imposition of foreign control. One of the most significant uprisings was the revolt of Ali Ben Ghedhahem in 1881-1882, which was brutally suppressed by the French military.

The interwar period witnessed the rise of organized nationalist movements seeking to challenge French domination and advocate for greater political and social rights for Tunisians. The Destour (Constitution) Party, founded in 1920, was one of the earliest nationalist movements, calling for constitutional reforms and greater autonomy for Tunisia. The party's moderate demands reflected the aspirations of the emerging Tunisian middle class, who sought to negotiate a more equitable relationship with the French authorities.

The rise of more radical nationalist movements in the 1930s and 1940s marked a significant shift in the struggle for independence. The Neo Destour Party, founded in 1934 by Habib Bourguiba and other young nationalists, adopted a more confrontational approach, demanding full independence and the end of French colonial rule. The party's leaders organized strikes, protests, and acts of civil disobedience to mobilize popular support and challenge the legitimacy of the colonial administration. The repression of these activities by the French authorities only served to galvanize the nationalist movement and increase its appeal among the broader population.

The outbreak of World War II and the subsequent German occupation of Tunisia in 1942-1943 further complicated the political situation. The wartime experience exposed the vulnerabilities of the French colonial regime and highlighted the potential for change. The post-war period saw renewed efforts by the nationalist movements to achieve independence, capitalizing on the weakened position of France and the broader decolonization trends sweeping across Africa and Asia.

The path to independence was marked by negotiations, conflicts, and compromises. The French government, under increasing pressure both domestically and internationally, began to make concessions to the nationalist demands. In 1954, the French Prime Minister Pierre Mendès-France announced a policy of gradual self-government for Tunisia. This policy culminated in the granting of internal autonomy to Tunisia in 1955, with Habib Bourguiba becoming the Prime Minister.

The final step towards full independence was achieved on March 20, 1956, when Tunisia officially became an independent nation.

Habib Bourguiba, the leader of the Neo Destour Party, was appointed the first Prime Minister, and later, the first President of Tunisia. The achievement of independence was a significant milestone, reflecting the determination and resilience of the Tunisian people in their struggle for self-determination and sovereignty.

The legacy of French influence in Tunisia is complex and multifaceted, encompassing both positive and negative aspects. On the positive side, the French colonial period brought about significant modernization and development in terms of infrastructure, education, and economic diversification. The introduction of Western education and legal systems contributed to the emergence of a modern Tunisian state with a well-defined administrative structure. The development of transportation and communication networks facilitated economic growth and integration into the global economy.

However, the negative aspects of French colonial rule cannot be overlooked. The economic exploitation, social inequalities, and cultural imposition left deep scars on Tunisian society. The expropriation of land, the forced labor practices, and the marginalization of the indigenous population created lasting economic and social disparities. The promotion of French language and culture at the expense of Tunisian identity led to a cultural dislocation that continued to influence post-independence policies and identity politics.

In the post-independence period, Tunisia embarked on a path of nation-building and economic development under the leadership of Habib Bourguiba. The new government implemented policies aimed at modernizing the economy, improving social services, and promoting national unity. Bourguiba's vision of a secular and progressive Tunisia guided the country's development, but also led to tensions with conservative and religious elements within society. The challenge of balancing modernization with the preservation of cultural identity remained a central theme in Tunisia's post-colonial journey.

The influence of French culture and institutions continued to be felt in Tunisia long after independence. The French language remained an important medium of instruction, administration, and commerce, reflecting the enduring legacy of colonial education policies. The legal and administrative systems introduced by the French provided a foundation for the new Tunisian state, although efforts were made to adapt and indigenize these institutions to reflect local realities and aspirations.

Chapter 46: Spanish Rule in Guatemala

The Spanish rule in Guatemala, lasting from the early 16th century until the early 19th century, is a crucial period that profoundly transformed the region's political, social, economic, and cultural landscape. The Spanish conquest of Guatemala was part of the broader Spanish colonization of the Americas, which began with Christopher Columbus's voyages in the late 15th century. This period in Guatemala was characterized by the subjugation and exploitation of indigenous populations, the imposition of European culture and religion, and significant changes in the economic and social structures of the region.

The Spanish conquest of Guatemala was initiated by the expeditions of Pedro de Alvarado, a lieutenant of Hernán Cortés, the conqueror of Mexico. Alvarado's first expedition to Guatemala began in 1523, following the successful conquest of the Aztec Empire. The initial phase of the conquest involved fierce battles with various indigenous groups, including the K'iche', Kaqchikel, and Tz'utujil peoples. These groups, part of the Maya civilization, had complex societies with advanced knowledge of astronomy, mathematics, and architecture. Despite their sophisticated societies, the indigenous populations were ultimately defeated due to a combination of Spanish military technology, European diseases to which the natives had no immunity, and internal divisions among the Maya groups.

Pedro de Alvarado's conquest culminated in the capture of the K'iche' capital of Q'umarkaj in 1524. Following the subjugation of the K'iche', Alvarado turned his attention to the neighboring Kaqchikel, initially forming an alliance with them against the K'iche'. However, this alliance was short-lived, and the Kaqchikel were soon subjugated as well. The conquest of the highland Maya was completed with the defeat of the Tz'utujil in 1525. The Spanish established their first settlement in Guatemala, Santiago de los Caballeros, in the present-day region of Iximche, which later moved to its present location in Antigua Guatemala.

The establishment of Spanish rule in Guatemala brought about significant changes in the political and administrative structures of the region. The Spanish imposed a colonial administration system that replaced the existing indigenous governance structures. This system was characterized by the encomienda system, in which Spanish conquistadors were granted control over land and the indigenous people living on it. The encomenderos, or holders of the encomiendas, were responsible for the protection and Christianization of the indigenous people in exchange for tribute and labor. This system led to widespread exploitation and abuse of the native population, with the encomenderos often prioritizing economic gain over the welfare of the indigenous people.

The Spanish colonial administration in Guatemala was also marked by the establishment of the audiencia, a high court that served as both a judicial and administrative body. The Real Audiencia of Guatemala, established in 1543, governed the Kingdom of Guatemala, which encompassed present-day Guatemala, Belize, Honduras, El Salvador, Nicaragua, and Costa Rica. The audiencia was based in Santiago de los Caballeros and was responsible for overseeing the administration of justice, taxation, and the implementation of royal policies. The establishment of the audiencia solidified Spanish control over the region and facilitated the integration of the various territories into the Spanish Empire.

The imposition of Spanish rule in Guatemala had profound economic implications for the region. The Spanish introduced new agricultural practices, crops, and livestock, transforming the local economy. The encomienda system facilitated the extraction of resources and the production of goods for export to Spain. The Spanish introduced crops such as wheat, sugarcane, and coffee, which became important cash crops in the colonial economy. Livestock, including cattle, horses, and sheep, were also introduced, leading to the development of ranching and altering the landscape and traditional agricultural practices.

The introduction of European agriculture and livestock had a significant impact on the indigenous population, whose traditional farming practices and land use were disrupted. The encomienda system and the demand for labor on plantations and in mines led to the forced labor and displacement of many indigenous people. The Spanish also imposed a tribute system, requiring indigenous communities to provide goods and labor to the colonial authorities. This system placed a heavy burden on the native population, contributing to widespread poverty and social dislocation.

In addition to economic exploitation, the Spanish conquest brought about significant cultural and religious changes. The Spanish were determined to convert the indigenous population to Christianity, and the Catholic Church played a central role in the colonization process. Missionaries, particularly Franciscans, Dominicans, and Jesuits, established missions and churches throughout Guatemala, often building them on the ruins of indigenous temples. The process of conversion was often coercive, involving the destruction of indigenous religious symbols and practices and the imposition of Catholic rituals and beliefs.

The Catholic Church became a powerful institution in colonial Guatemala, influencing not only religious life but also education, social services, and governance. The establishment of schools and the introduction of European education were part of the broader effort to assimilate the indigenous population into Spanish colonial society. Despite the efforts of the missionaries, indigenous religious practices persisted, often blending with Catholic rituals to create syncretic forms of worship that are still present in contemporary Guatemalan culture.

The impact of Spanish rule on the indigenous population was devastating. The introduction of European diseases, such as smallpox, measles, and influenza, to which the indigenous people had no immunity, led to catastrophic population declines. It is estimated that up to 90% of the indigenous population perished within the first century of Spanish rule, primarily due to disease, but also as a result of violence, forced labor, and social disruption. The drastic reduction in the indigenous population had far-reaching consequences for the social and economic structures of the region.

Despite the harsh conditions imposed by Spanish rule, indigenous resistance and resilience were notable features of this period. Indigenous communities employed various forms of resistance, ranging from armed rebellion to passive resistance and negotiation. Notable uprisings, such as the revolt led by the Kaqchikel leader Tecún Umán in the early years of the conquest and later rebellions in the 16th and 17th centuries, demonstrated the determination of the indigenous people to resist foreign domination. Over time, indigenous communities adapted to the new colonial order, finding ways to preserve their cultural identity and autonomy within the constraints of Spanish rule.

The Bourbon Reforms of the 18th century, initiated by the Spanish crown, brought about significant changes in the administration and economy of colonial Guatemala. These reforms aimed to centralize and modernize the colonial administration, increase revenue, and reduce corruption. The establishment of new administrative divisions, the creation of intendancies, and the promotion of economic diversification were key components of the reforms. The Bourbon Reforms also sought to reduce the power of the Catholic Church and increase royal control over colonial affairs.

The implementation of the Bourbon Reforms in Guatemala led to increased tensions between the colonial authorities and the local population. The reforms disrupted established economic and social structures, leading to resistance from both the indigenous population and the Creole elite. The increased taxation and labor demands imposed by the reforms exacerbated existing grievances and contributed to social unrest. The reforms also led to a decline in the power and influence of the traditional encomenderos, as the crown sought to reduce their control over the indigenous population and increase direct royal administration.

The late 18th and early 19th centuries saw the rise of independence movements throughout Latin America, influenced by the Enlightenment ideas of liberty, equality, and self-determination. The events of the Napoleonic Wars in Europe, particularly the occupation of Spain by Napoleon and the abdication of King Ferdinand VII, created a power vacuum and provided an opportunity for colonial subjects to assert their demands for independence. In Central America, including Guatemala, the drive for independence was fueled by a combination of local grievances, economic interests, and the influence of independence movements in neighboring regions.

The path to independence in Guatemala was marked by a series of political and military events that culminated in the declaration of independence from Spain on September 15, 1821. This declaration was part of a broader movement for independence in Central America, which saw the creation of the United Provinces of Central America, a federation that included present-day Guatemala, El Salvador, Honduras, Nicaragua, and Costa Rica. However, the federation was short-lived, plagued by internal conflicts and regional rivalries, leading to its dissolution in 1838. Guatemala, along with the other member states, became an independent republic.

The legacy of Spanish rule in Guatemala is complex and multifaceted, encompassing both positive and negative aspects. On the positive side, the Spanish introduced new technologies, agricultural practices, and infrastructure that contributed to the economic development of the region. The establishment of cities, roads, and ports facilitated trade and communication, laying the groundwork for future growth. The introduction of European education and legal systems also provided a foundation for the modern Guatemalan state.

However, the negative impacts of Spanish colonization were profound and long-lasting. The conquest and colonization resulted in the destruction of indigenous civilizations, the loss of life, and the exploitation and marginalization of the native population. The imposition of the encomienda system and other forms of forced labor led to widespread poverty and social inequality. The cultural imposition of Catholicism and European values disrupted indigenous traditions and identities, creating a legacy of cultural dislocation that continues to influence Guatemalan society.

The post-independence period in Guatemala was characterized by continued struggles for power, social justice, and economic development. The legacy of Spanish colonial rule, with its entrenched social hierarchies and economic disparities, created significant challenges for the new republic. Efforts to address these challenges have been ongoing, with varying degrees of success, as Guatemala continues to navigate the complexities of its colonial past and its aspirations for a more just and equitable future.

Chapter 47: British Colonization of New Zealand

The British colonization of New Zealand is a complex and multifaceted chapter in the history of the Pacific, spanning from the late 18th century to the mid-20th century. This period was marked by exploration, cultural exchanges, conflicts, treaties, and profound transformations in the political, social, and economic landscape of New Zealand. The interactions between the indigenous Māori population and the British colonizers were characterized by both cooperation and conflict, leading to significant changes that continue to shape the country's identity today.

The first recorded European contact with New Zealand occurred in 1642 when the Dutch explorer Abel Tasman arrived on the western coast of the South Island. However, it wasn't until the voyages of British explorer Captain James Cook in 1769-1770 that detailed maps and accounts of New Zealand were created, sparking European interest in the region. Cook's expeditions provided valuable information about the geography, flora, fauna, and Māori inhabitants of New Zealand. His encounters with the Māori were generally peaceful, although there were some instances of violence and misunderstanding.

Following Cook's voyages, European whalers, sealers, and traders began to visit New Zealand regularly in the late 18th and early 19th centuries. These early European visitors established trading relationships with the Māori, exchanging goods such as firearms, metal tools, and textiles for food, timber, and flax. The introduction of European goods had a significant impact on Māori society, leading to changes in social structures, warfare, and economic activities. Firearms, in particular, altered the balance of power among different Māori tribes, leading to a period of intense intertribal warfare known as the Musket Wars (1807-1845).

The increasing presence of European traders and settlers in New Zealand led to growing concerns about lawlessness and conflicts between Māori and Europeans. In response, British missionaries, particularly from the Church Missionary Society, began to establish missions in New Zealand in the early 19th century. These missionaries aimed to convert the Māori to Christianity and promote European values and practices. The missionaries played a significant role in mediating between Māori and European settlers, advocating for Māori rights, and introducing written language to the Māori through the translation of the Bible and other texts.

The British government's interest in formally annexing New Zealand grew in the 1830s due to several factors, including the increasing number of British settlers, the strategic importance of New Zealand in the Pacific, and concerns about French intentions in the region. In 1833, James Busby was appointed as the British Resident in New Zealand, tasked with protecting British interests and mediating conflicts between Māori and Europeans. However, Busby's position was limited in authority and resources, and he struggled to maintain order.

The turning point in the British colonization of New Zealand came with the signing of the Treaty of Waitangi on February 6, 1840. The treaty was negotiated between representatives of the British Crown, led by Captain William Hobson, and various Māori chiefs from the North Island. The Treaty of Waitangi is often considered New Zealand's founding document, establishing the framework for British sovereignty and the relationship between the Crown and the Māori.

The Treaty of Waitangi consisted of three articles, each addressing different aspects of the relationship between the British and the Māori. The first article ceded sovereignty to the British Crown, while the second article guaranteed Māori the full, exclusive, and undisturbed possession of their lands, forests, fisheries, and other properties. The third article promised Māori the rights and privileges of British subjects. However, there were significant differences between the English and Māori versions of the treaty, leading to misunderstandings and disputes over its interpretation and implementation.

Following the signing of the Treaty of Waitangi, New Zealand was formally declared a British colony, and Hobson became the first Governor. The establishment of British rule brought significant changes to New Zealand's political and legal systems. The colonial government introduced British laws, established courts, and created administrative structures to govern the growing settler population and regulate interactions with the Māori. The colonial administration also promoted European settlement through land sales and immigration schemes, leading to a rapid increase in the number of British settlers.

The influx of European settlers and the demand for land led to tensions and conflicts with the Māori, who were often unwilling to sell their land or were dissatisfied with the terms of land transactions. The colonial government and settlers frequently resorted to dubious and coercive practices to acquire land, leading to widespread dispossession and marginalization of the Māori. These tensions culminated in a series of armed conflicts known as the New Zealand Wars (1845-1872), which were fought between various Māori iwi (tribes) and the British colonial forces, often with the support of settler militias.

The New Zealand Wars were marked by several key conflicts, including the Northern War (1845-1846), the Taranaki Wars (1860-1861, 1863-1866), and the Waikato War (1863-1864). The wars resulted in significant loss of life and property on both sides, with the Māori suffering particularly heavy casualties and land confiscations. The British victory in these conflicts and the subsequent confiscation of large tracts of Māori land had a devastating impact on Māori communities, leading to economic hardship, social disintegration, and loss of cultural heritage.

In the latter half of the 19th century, the British colonial administration implemented policies aimed at assimilating the Māori into European society. These policies included the promotion of English language education, the suppression of Māori customs and practices, and the encouragement of European farming methods. The Native Schools Act of 1867 established a system of state-funded schools for Māori children, with the curriculum focused on English language and European subjects. The education system was a tool of assimilation, seeking to integrate Māori into the colonial economy and society while eroding their cultural identity.

Despite these assimilationist policies, the Māori demonstrated remarkable resilience and adaptability. They engaged with the colonial legal and political systems to assert their rights and protect their interests. Prominent Māori leaders, such as Wiremu Kingi, Te Whiti o Rongomai, and Tāwhiao, emerged as influential figures in the resistance against land confiscations and the defense of Māori autonomy. The establishment of the Māori King Movement (Kīngitanga) in the 1850s was a significant expression of Māori unity and resistance, with the aim of establishing an independent Māori nation within New Zealand.

The turn of the 20th century saw gradual changes in the relationship between the Māori and the colonial government. The introduction of representative government and the extension of the franchise to Māori men in 1867 provided Māori with a platform to participate in the political process. The establishment of the Māori Parliament (Te Kotahitanga) in the 1890s was another important development, allowing Māori leaders to advocate for their rights and promote self-governance.

The early 20th century also witnessed efforts to address the grievances of the Māori through legislative and judicial means. The establishment of the Native Land Court in 1865 aimed to individualize Māori land ownership and facilitate land sales, but it often led to further alienation of Māori land. In response to these issues, the government introduced measures such as the Native Lands Act of

1909, which sought to protect remaining Māori land and promote its development for the benefit of Māori communities.

The interwar period and the post-World War II era brought significant social and economic changes to New Zealand. The Māori urban migration, driven by the search for employment and better living conditions, led to the growth of Māori communities in urban centers. This migration resulted in the blending of Māori and European cultures and the emergence of new forms of Māori identity and activism. The Māori Women's Welfare League, founded in 1951, played a crucial role in addressing social issues and advocating for Māori rights.

The latter half of the 20th century saw a resurgence of Māori cultural and political activism. The Māori Renaissance of the 1970s and 1980s was marked by a renewed interest in Māori language, culture, and traditions. The establishment of the Waitangi Tribunal in 1975 provided a legal mechanism for addressing historical grievances related to the Treaty of Waitangi. The tribunal's findings and recommendations have led to various settlements and compensations for Māori iwi, contributing to the ongoing process of reconciliation and redress.

In contemporary New Zealand, the legacy of British colonization continues to influence the country's political, social, and cultural dynamics. The Treaty of Waitangi remains a foundational document, enshrining the principles of partnership, protection, and participation between the Crown and the Māori. The recognition of Māori rights and the promotion of biculturalism are central to New Zealand's national identity and governance.

The British colonization of New Zealand was a period of profound change, marked by the imposition of European political and legal systems, the transformation of the economy, and significant social and cultural upheaval. The interactions between the British and the Māori were characterized by both cooperation and conflict, leading to enduring legacies that continue to shape New Zealand's society and identity. The resilience and adaptability of the Māori people in the face of colonization have been crucial in preserving their culture and asserting their rights, contributing to the rich and diverse fabric of contemporary New Zealand.

Chapter 48: Dutch Colonization of Taiwan

The Dutch colonization of Taiwan, also known as Formosa, is a fascinating episode in the history of European colonialism in Asia, spanning from 1624 to 1662. The Dutch East India Company (VOC) established a presence on the island to enhance its trade network in East Asia, driven by the strategic and economic advantages that Taiwan offered. This period of Dutch rule profoundly impacted the indigenous population, the economic development of the island, and the geopolitical dynamics of the region.

The Dutch East India Company was a powerful maritime trading entity in the 17th century, aiming to dominate the spice trade and establish trading posts across Asia. Taiwan, situated off the southeastern coast of China, became an attractive target due to its strategic location along major maritime trade routes and its potential as a base for trade with China, Japan, and Southeast Asia. Prior to the Dutch arrival, Taiwan was inhabited by various indigenous Austronesian tribes, each with its own distinct culture, language, and social structure. These tribes engaged in agriculture, fishing, and trade with neighboring regions, including the Chinese mainland.

The Dutch initially attempted to establish a foothold in the Pescadores Islands (Penghu) in 1622 but faced resistance from the Ming Dynasty, which controlled the region. After negotiations, the Dutch agreed to withdraw from the Pescadores and were granted permission to establish a trading post on Taiwan. In 1624, the Dutch established Fort Zeelandia on the southwestern coast of Taiwan, near present-day Tainan. This fort became the administrative and military center of Dutch operations on the island.

Fort Zeelandia was strategically located on a natural harbor, facilitating the establishment of trade links with the Chinese mainland,

Japan, and other parts of Asia. The Dutch quickly began to develop the area around the fort, constructing buildings, fortifications, and infrastructure to support their colonial endeavors. The VOC aimed to exploit Taiwan's resources, including deer hides, sugar, rice, and other agricultural products, to enhance its profitability.

The Dutch colonization of Taiwan was marked by significant interactions with the indigenous population. The Dutch sought to establish control over the indigenous tribes and integrate them into the colonial economy. They employed a combination of military force, diplomacy, and economic incentives to achieve this goal. The VOC established a system of alliances and treaties with various tribes, encouraging them to trade with the Dutch and adopt European agricultural practices. The Dutch introduced new crops, such as sugarcane and tobacco, and provided tools and training to improve agricultural productivity.

The relationship between the Dutch and the indigenous tribes was complex and varied across different regions of the island. In some areas, the Dutch managed to establish relatively peaceful and cooperative relationships with the tribes, integrating them into the colonial economy and encouraging intermarriage with European settlers. In other areas, the Dutch faced resistance from tribes unwilling to submit to foreign rule. Conflicts and uprisings occurred periodically, necessitating military expeditions to subdue rebellious tribes and assert Dutch authority.

One of the most significant aspects of Dutch rule in Taiwan was the introduction of a new legal and administrative system. The VOC established a colonial government with a governor at the head, supported by a council of officials responsible for various aspects of administration, justice, and trade. The Dutch introduced European legal principles and practices, creating courts to adjudicate disputes and enforce colonial laws. This legal system coexisted with indigenous customary laws, leading to a complex legal landscape where different legal traditions interacted and influenced each other.

The Dutch also made efforts to convert the indigenous population to Christianity, viewing religious conversion as a means to strengthen their control and integrate the indigenous people into the colonial society. Missionaries from the Dutch Reformed Church were sent to Taiwan to establish churches, schools, and mission stations. They translated religious texts into local languages, taught European customs and values, and attempted to eradicate indigenous religious practices. While some indigenous people converted to Christianity, the overall impact of missionary efforts was limited, and traditional beliefs and practices persisted in many areas.

Economically, the Dutch colonization of Taiwan had a significant impact on the island's development. The VOC introduced new agricultural techniques, crops, and livestock, transforming the local economy and increasing agricultural productivity. The Dutch established sugar plantations and mills, encouraging the production of sugar for export to markets in Asia and Europe. They also promoted the cultivation of rice, tobacco, and other cash crops, integrating Taiwan into the broader network of global trade.

Trade played a central role in the Dutch colonial economy in Taiwan. The VOC established trading posts and warehouses to facilitate the exchange of goods between Taiwan and other parts of Asia. Taiwanese products, such as deer hides, sugar, and rice, were exported to China, Japan, and Southeast Asia, while the Dutch imported silk, porcelain, spices, and other goods for resale in European markets. The Dutch monopoly on trade with Japan, through the port of Hirado and later Dejima, further enhanced the profitability of their operations in Taiwan.

The Dutch colonization of Taiwan also had significant demographic effects. The VOC encouraged the settlement of Dutch and other European settlers on the island, as well as the migration of

Chinese laborers and traders from the mainland. This influx of settlers and laborers led to the growth of new towns and settlements, creating a more diverse and cosmopolitan society. The intermingling of different cultures and ethnicities contributed to the development of a unique colonial society with a blend of European, Chinese, and indigenous influences.

Despite the economic and administrative successes of the Dutch colonization, the VOC faced numerous challenges and threats to its control over Taiwan. The most significant challenge came from the Ming loyalist and pirate leader Koxinga (Zheng Chenggong), who sought to overthrow the Qing Dynasty and restore the Ming Dynasty. Koxinga viewed Taiwan as a strategic base for his operations and launched a campaign to expel the Dutch from the island.

In 1661, Koxinga's forces laid siege to Fort Zeelandia, cutting off supplies and bombarding the fort. The siege lasted for nine months, during which the Dutch defenders, led by Governor Frederick Coyett, endured severe hardships. Despite their efforts to negotiate and resist, the Dutch were ultimately forced to surrender in February 1662. The fall of Fort Zeelandia marked the end of Dutch rule in Taiwan, and Koxinga established his own regime on the island, which lasted until the Qing Dynasty annexed Taiwan in 1683.

The Dutch colonization of Taiwan had lasting legacies, both positive and negative. On the positive side, the Dutch introduced new agricultural practices, crops, and technologies that contributed to the island's economic development. The establishment of trade links with China, Japan, and other parts of Asia integrated Taiwan into the global economy and facilitated cultural exchanges. The introduction of European legal and administrative systems, as well as Christian missionary efforts, left an enduring impact on Taiwanese society.

However, the negative aspects of Dutch colonization were also significant. The imposition of foreign rule and exploitation of indigenous resources led to conflicts and resistance from the indigenous population. The introduction of European diseases, to which the indigenous people had no immunity, resulted in significant population declines. The forced labor and land confiscations disrupted traditional livelihoods and social structures, leading to economic hardship and social dislocation for many indigenous communities.

The end of Dutch rule did not erase the impact of their colonization. The period of Dutch rule remains a significant chapter in Taiwan's history, shaping the island's development and influencing subsequent colonial and modern eras. The legacy of Dutch colonization is reflected in place names, architectural styles, and cultural practices that persist in Taiwan to this day.

Chapter 49: Italian Colonization of Somalia

The Italian colonization of Somalia, part of the broader phenomenon of European imperialism in Africa, spanned from the late 19th century until the mid-20th century. This period was marked by various phases of military conquest, administrative consolidation, economic exploitation, and socio-cultural transformation. The impact of Italian rule on Somalia's political, economic, and social structures has left a lasting legacy, influencing the country's post-colonial development and contemporary challenges.

The scramble for Africa in the late 19th century saw European powers aggressively expanding their empires by claiming territories across the continent. Italy, seeking to join the ranks of other colonial powers and enhance its international prestige, turned its attention to the Horn of Africa. The area that would become Italian Somaliland was strategically significant due to its location along the Indian Ocean and its proximity to the Red Sea, providing potential access to maritime trade routes.

Italy's initial incursions into the region began in the 1880s with the signing of various treaties with local Somali sultans and clan leaders. These treaties often involved promises of protection and mutual cooperation, though they were frequently misunderstood or manipulated by the Italians to assert greater control over the territory. In 1889, Italy formally established a protectorate over parts of northern Somalia, known as Italian Somaliland, and began to expand its influence through both diplomacy and military force.

The early years of Italian colonization were marked by efforts to establish control over the diverse and often resistant Somali population. The Italians faced significant challenges in subjugating the fiercely independent Somali clans, who were accustomed to a decentralized political structure and had a long history of resisting foreign domination. To consolidate their authority, the Italians employed a combination of military campaigns, punitive expeditions, and strategic alliances with compliant local leaders.

One of the most significant conflicts during this period was the Dervish movement, led by Mohammed Abdullah Hassan, also known as the "Mad Mullah." Hassan's movement, which began in the late 19th century, aimed to resist foreign (including Italian and British) influence and establish a Somali Islamic state. The Dervish forces waged a protracted guerrilla war against the colonial powers, conducting raids, ambushes, and hit-and-run attacks. The Italian military struggled to suppress the Dervish uprising, which continued sporadically until Hassan's death in 1920 and the eventual defeat of the Dervish forces.

By the early 20th century, Italy had established a more stable colonial administration in Somalia. The colonial government implemented policies aimed at consolidating its control and exploiting the region's economic resources. Infrastructure development, including the construction of roads, ports, and railways, was a priority to facilitate the extraction and export of agricultural products and other commodities. The Italians introduced new agricultural techniques and crops, promoting the cultivation of bananas, sugarcane, and cotton for export markets.

The economic policies of the colonial administration were geared towards the benefit of the Italian metropole, often at the expense of the local Somali population. Large tracts of fertile land were appropriated for Italian settlers and agricultural enterprises, displacing Somali pastoralists and farmers. The introduction of cash crops and the focus on export-oriented agriculture disrupted traditional subsistence practices and altered the socio-economic landscape of the region.

In addition to economic exploitation, the Italian colonization of Somalia involved significant social and cultural changes. The colonial government implemented policies aimed at assimilating the Somali population into Italian culture and values. Education was a key tool in this process, with the establishment of schools that taught Italian language, history, and customs. The Italians also promoted Christianity, although their efforts to convert the predominantly Muslim Somali population were largely unsuccessful.

The impact of Italian cultural policies was uneven, with urban areas experiencing greater degrees of assimilation than rural regions. In the cities, particularly in the colonial capital of Mogadishu, the Italian influence was more pronounced, with the construction of European-style buildings, the introduction of Italian cuisine, and the establishment of social and recreational institutions catering to Italian settlers and Somali elites. In contrast, rural areas remained more resistant to cultural assimilation, maintaining traditional practices and social structures.

The period of Italian colonization also saw the implementation of repressive measures aimed at maintaining control and suppressing dissent. The colonial administration established a system of forced labor, conscripting Somalis to work on infrastructure projects, plantations, and other enterprises. The harsh working conditions, coupled with the lack of adequate compensation and respect for laborers' rights, led to widespread suffering and resentment among the local population. Resistance to colonial rule persisted in various forms, including passive resistance, protests, and occasional uprisings.

The onset of World War II brought significant changes to the Italian colonial presence in Somalia. In 1940, Italian forces launched an invasion of British Somaliland, temporarily expanding their control over the region. However, the tide of the war soon turned against the Axis powers, and by 1941, British and Allied forces had recaptured British Somaliland and occupied Italian Somaliland. The defeat of Italy in the war marked the end of its colonial rule in Somalia.

Following the war, Italian Somaliland came under British military administration before being placed under United Nations trusteeship in 1950, with Italy as the administering authority. This period, known as the Trusteeship Administration, was intended to prepare Somalia for eventual independence. The UN trusteeship was characterized by efforts to develop infrastructure, improve education, and promote economic development, although many of the underlying issues from the colonial period persisted.

On July 1, 1960, Somalia achieved independence, with the former British Somaliland and Italian Somaliland territories uniting to form the Somali Republic. The legacy of Italian colonization, however, continued to influence the newly independent nation. The political and administrative structures established during the colonial period, as well as the socio-economic disparities and divisions, presented significant challenges for the post-colonial government.

The impact of Italian colonization on Somalia's development has been the subject of extensive analysis and debate. On one hand, the infrastructure and economic initiatives introduced during the colonial period contributed to the modernization of the region and laid the groundwork for future development. The establishment of educational institutions, the introduction of new agricultural techniques, and the development of transportation networks facilitated economic growth and integration into the global economy.

On the other hand, the exploitative and repressive policies of the colonial administration left a legacy of economic inequality, social dislocation, and political instability. The appropriation of land for Italian settlers and enterprises disrupted traditional livelihoods and contributed to enduring land disputes and conflicts. The forced labor system and the suppression of dissent fostered deep-seated resentment and resistance among the Somali population.

Moreover, the cultural policies of the colonial administration, aimed at assimilating Somalis into Italian culture, had mixed and often detrimental effects. While some segments of the population, particularly in urban areas, adopted aspects of Italian culture and education, the broader impact was a weakening of traditional social structures and cultural practices. The emphasis on Italian language and customs in education and administration created a cultural divide between the colonized population and their colonial rulers.

The post-colonial period in Somalia has been marked by efforts to address the legacy of colonial rule and build a cohesive and stable nation-state. However, the challenges inherited from the colonial period, including economic disparities, social divisions, and political instability, have continued to pose significant obstacles. The civil war and state collapse that engulfed Somalia in the late 20th and early 21st centuries can be traced, in part, to the unresolved issues and grievances stemming from the colonial era.

In recent years, there has been a renewed interest in examining and understanding the history of Italian colonization in Somalia. Scholars, historians, and policymakers have sought to explore the complexities of this period, including the interactions between the colonizers and the colonized, the impact of colonial policies on Somali society, and the long-term consequences for the region's development. This historical analysis is crucial for informing contemporary efforts to promote reconciliation, development, and stability in Somalia.

Chapter 50: British Influence in Fiji

The British influence in Fiji is a complex and multifaceted chapter in the island nation's history, spanning from the early 19th century until Fiji's independence in 1970. This period was marked by profound changes in Fiji's political, social, and economic structures, driven by British colonial policies and practices. The impact of British rule has left an indelible mark on Fiji's development and continues to influence its contemporary society.

The early interactions between the British and Fiji were largely driven by the interests of traders, missionaries, and settlers. In the early 1800s, European explorers and traders began arriving in the Fiji Islands, drawn by the region's abundant natural resources and strategic location in the Pacific Ocean. These early contacts were often fraught with tension and conflict, as Fijian chiefs and European newcomers vied for control over trade and territory.

One of the significant early British influences in Fiji was the introduction of Christianity by missionaries. The London Missionary Society, followed by other missionary organizations, established missions in Fiji in the early 19th century. The missionaries sought to convert the Fijian population to Christianity, often facing resistance from traditional chiefs and communities. Over time, however, Christianity took root, and by the mid-19th century, it had become a major force in Fijian society, leading to significant cultural and social changes.

The process of British colonization formally began in the mid-19th century, driven by geopolitical and economic considerations. In 1874, following a period of internal strife and conflict among Fijian chiefs, Fiji was ceded to the British Crown. This cession was formalized through a deed of cession signed by a number of Fijian chiefs, including Seru Epenisa Cakobau, who had previously declared himself King of Fiji in an attempt to unify the islands. The British established a colonial administration with a governor at its head, supported by a bureaucracy that sought to implement British policies and maintain order.

One of the key aspects of British colonial policy in Fiji was the establishment of a plantation economy. The British aimed to transform Fiji into a major producer of sugarcane, leveraging the fertile land and favorable climate of the islands. To support this economic model, the colonial administration encouraged the establishment of sugar plantations, attracting British and other European investors. The development of the sugar industry required a large labor force, which led to the introduction of indentured laborers from India.

The indentured labor system, which began in 1879, brought thousands of Indian laborers to Fiji to work on the sugar plantations. These laborers were contracted for fixed terms, usually five years, after which they could choose to return to India or remain in Fiji. The conditions for the indentured laborers were harsh, with long hours, low wages, and inadequate living conditions. Despite the hardships, many Indian laborers chose to remain in Fiji after their contracts ended, leading to the establishment of a significant Indo-Fijian community.

The introduction of Indian laborers and the growth of the Indo-Fijian population had far-reaching social and demographic impacts on Fiji. The Indo-Fijians brought with them their own cultural, religious, and social practices, contributing to the cultural diversity of the islands. However, the colonial policies also fostered divisions between the indigenous Fijian population and the Indo-Fijians, laying the groundwork for ethnic tensions that would persist into the post-colonial period.

British colonial rule in Fiji also involved significant changes to the traditional Fijian social and political structures. The colonial administration sought to integrate the indigenous Fijian chiefs into the colonial system, establishing a system of indirect rule. The chiefs were granted certain administrative powers and responsibilities, and the colonial government relied on their cooperation to implement policies and maintain control. This system of indirect rule helped to preserve some aspects of traditional Fijian authority, but it also altered the dynamics of power and governance within Fijian society.

The British colonial administration implemented a range of policies aimed at modernizing Fiji's infrastructure and economy. Roads, ports, and other infrastructure were developed to support the plantation economy and facilitate trade. Education and healthcare systems were introduced, albeit primarily to serve the needs of the colonial economy and the European settlers. The colonial government also introduced new legal and administrative systems, which were based on British models but adapted to the local context.

The impact of British colonial policies on the indigenous Fijian population was profound. The introduction of a cash economy and the emphasis on plantation agriculture disrupted traditional subsistence practices and social structures. Land policies implemented by the colonial administration resulted in the alienation of significant portions of Fijian land for use by European settlers and plantation owners. While some land was reserved for indigenous use, the loss of land and the imposition of new economic systems had lasting effects on Fijian society.

During the colonial period, Fiji's political landscape was shaped by the interests and priorities of the British administration. The colonial government sought to maintain control and stability, often at the expense of democratic participation and representation. The colonial administration was characterized by a hierarchical and paternalistic approach, with decisions made by British officials and limited input from the local population. This lack of political representation and participation would become a significant issue in the later stages of the colonial period and the push for independence.

The period following World War II saw increasing demands for political reform and greater autonomy in many British colonies, including Fiji. The global movement towards decolonization and the changing political dynamics within the British Empire created an environment in which the push for independence gained momentum. In Fiji, political movements and parties began to emerge, advocating for greater representation and self-governance.

One of the key political figures in the push for Fijian independence was Ratu Sir Kamisese Mara, a prominent Fijian chief and statesman. Mara played a central role in negotiating the terms of independence and in shaping the post-colonial political landscape of Fiji. The process of decolonization culminated in Fiji's independence on October 10, 1970. The transition to independence was relatively peaceful, with a constitution that sought to balance the interests of the indigenous Fijian population and the Indo-Fijian community.

The legacy of British colonial rule in Fiji has been a subject of extensive analysis and debate. On one hand, British colonial policies and infrastructure development contributed to the modernization of Fiji, laying the groundwork for its post-colonial economy and state institutions. The introduction of new agricultural practices, education, and healthcare systems had lasting impacts on Fijian society. The establishment of a legal and administrative framework provided a foundation for the post-independence government.

On the other hand, the colonial period also left a legacy of economic inequality, social division, and political challenges. The plantation economy and land policies disrupted traditional livelihoods and contributed to enduring disparities in land ownership and economic opportunities. The introduction of the indentured labor system and the resulting demographic changes fostered ethnic tensions that have continued to shape Fijian politics and society. The system of indirect rule and the hierarchical nature of the colonial administration limited political participation and representation, creating challenges for the development of a democratic and inclusive political system.

The post-colonial period in Fiji has been marked by efforts to address the legacy of colonial rule and build a cohesive and stable nation. The political landscape has been characterized by tensions and conflicts between different ethnic groups, particularly between indigenous Fijians and Indo-Fijians. These tensions have been reflected in political instability, including coups and changes in government. Efforts to promote reconciliation, development, and inclusivity have been ongoing, with varying degrees of success.

In recent years, there has been a renewed interest in examining and understanding the history of British colonial rule in Fiji. Scholars, historians, and policymakers have sought to explore the complexities of this period, including the interactions between the colonizers and the colonized, the impact of colonial policies on Fijian society, and the long-term consequences for the region's development. This historical analysis is crucial for informing contemporary efforts to promote reconciliation, development, and stability in Fiji.

Epilogue

As we conclude our journey through the annals of history, "The Footprints of Colonialism: Tracing the Impact of Imperial Rule," we find ourselves at a juncture of reflection and understanding. The chapters have taken us across continents and centuries, revealing the multifaceted impact of colonialism on diverse societies and cultures. From the shores of Africa to the islands of the Pacific, from the bustling cities of Asia to the vast landscapes of the Americas, the legacy of imperial rule is etched into the fabric of our world.

Colonialism, with its complex interplay of power and resistance, has left a profound and lasting impact on the global order. It has shaped nations, economies, and identities, creating both opportunities and challenges that continue to resonate today. The stories of exploitation and oppression are intertwined with tales of resilience, adaptation, and resistance. These narratives remind us of the human capacity for both cruelty and compassion, for destruction and creation.

The echoes of colonialism are still felt in contemporary geopolitics, economic disparities, and cultural dynamics. Many of the challenges faced by post-colonial nations—such as poverty, political instability, and social inequality—are rooted in the historical injustices of imperial rule. Yet, the legacy of colonialism is not solely one of suffering. It has also spurred movements for independence, self-determination, and social justice, leading to significant strides towards equality and human rights.

As we stand at this point in history, it is crucial to recognize that the legacy of colonialism is not static. It continues to evolve, influenced by the ongoing struggles and aspirations of people around the world. The process of decolonization is far from complete, and the pursuit of justice and reconciliation remains an urgent task. By understanding the past, we equip ourselves to address the injustices of the present and build a more equitable future.

This book is a testament to the importance of historical memory. It calls on us to remember the lessons of the past and to honor the experiences of those who lived through the trials of colonialism. It encourages us to engage with history critically and compassionately, recognizing the interconnectedness of our global community.

As we move forward, let us carry with us the stories and insights gained from this exploration. Let us strive to create a world where the legacy of colonialism serves not as a burden, but as a catalyst for positive change. By acknowledging the complexities of our shared history, we can work towards a future marked by understanding, justice, and mutual respect.

Thank you for embarking on this journey through "The Footprints of Colonialism: Tracing the Impact of Imperial Rule." May the insights gained here inspire us all to contribute to a more just and equitable world.

The End.